PRAISE FOR WORK WITH ME!

"*Work with Me!* is an excellent tool to use in resolving workplace dissention. This book prepares the reader with a step-by-step process that really works! Using Scott's Emotion-Reason-Intuition (ERI) model to diffuse and resolve conflict ensures that each person's needs are met. As a trained conflict resolution mediator, I recommend *Work with Me!*"

> Francie Koehler, criminal defense specialist,
> Special Circumstances

"Gini Graham Scott writes in a clear, professional style without sacrificing interest. She explains the processes of her model without jargon, illustrating them with numerous common workplace conflicts. I recommend *Work with Me!* as a good resource tool for managing conflict in work settings."

> Jim Garrison, Publications Coordinator,
> Community Boards, San Francisco

"As an organization consultant who specializes in reducing workplace conflict, I found that *Work with Me!* contains many useful conflict management techniques plus a good overall framework in the ERI model."

> Michael H. Smith, Ph.D.

"I found *Work with Me!* quite enlightening for my own business practices as a private investigator dealing with the diversity and complexity of information and people."

> Sam Brown, The Sam Brown Group, Inc.

"Gini Graham Scott's ERI model not only is a practical method for resolving conflicts, it also is easy for anyone to apply. As a conflict mediator and executive coach, I highly recommend this book to all managers and teams."

> Marilyn Manning, Ph.D., author of *Leadership Skills for Women*
> and *One-Stop Guide to Workshops*

"*Work with Me!* is a hands-on guide that can help any manager in any business. Every manager wants to have a positive atmosphere in the workplace, and this approach to resolving conflict is a great way to achieve it."

Dale Marie Golden, Assistant Vice President
and Branch Manager, Wells Fargo Bank

"As an executive speech coach, I find the methods and techniques in *Work with Me!* valuable for recommending to my clients, who often have to deal with conflicts as the heads or managers of large companies. The discussion of how to deal with difficult people and the ideas for coming up with alternative solutions to resolve conflict are especially useful."

Brenda Besdansky, Speakers World

ALSO BY GINI GRAHAM SCOTT

Resolving Conflict with Others and Within Yourself
The Empowered Mind: How to Harness the Creative Force Within You
Making Ethical Choices, Resolving Ethical Dilemmas
Mind Power: Picture Your Way to Success in Business
Effective Selling and Sales Management
Get Rich Through Multi-Level Selling
The Small Business Credit and Collection Guide
Collect Your Court Judgment
Success in Multi-Level Marketing
Can We Talk? The Power and Influence of Talk Shows

WORK WITH ME!

WORK WITH ME!

*Resolving Everyday
Conflict in Your
Organization*

GINI GRAHAM SCOTT

·D|B· DAVIES-BLACK PUBLISHING
Palo Alto, California

PUBLISHED BY
Davies-Black Publishing,
an imprint of Consulting Psychologists Press, Inc.
3803 East Bayshore Road
Palo Alto, CA 94303
800-624-1765

Special discounts on bulk quantities of Davies-Black books are available to corporations, professional associations, and other organizations. For details, contact the Director of Book Sales at Davies-Black Publishing, an imprint of Consulting Psychologists Press, Inc., 3803 East Bayshore Road, Palo Alto, CA 94303; 650-691-9123; Fax 650-623-9271.

Visit the Davies-Black Publishing web site at www.daviesblack.com.

04 03 02 01 00 10 9 8 7 6 5 4 3 2 1
Printed in the United States of America

Library of Congress Cataloging-in-Publication Data
Scott, Gini Graham
    Work with me! : resolving everyday conflict in your organization /
    Gini Graham Scott—1st ed.
        p. cm.
    Includes bibliographical references and index.
    ISBN 0-89106-137-1
    1. Conflict management. 2. Psychology, Industrial. 3. Organizational
    behavior. I. Title.
HD42 .S36 2000
658.4′053—dc21

                                                                99-057254

FIRST EDITION
First printing 2000

*To the many company owners, managers, and employees
who shared their everyday conflicts with me*

CONTENTS

CHARTS, FIGURES, AND WORKSHEETS

PREFACE

Difficult situations, which include conflicts, come up naturally and inevitably in every workplace and organization. They happen because people have different interests, goals, and priorities, or because resources are limited, or because there are communication problems, power struggles, mistaken perceptions and assumptions, and personality clashes. They also happen because some people are simply difficult to work with.

Work with Me! presents a new model for helping you solve problems and create a more satisfying work environment. Whatever your role at work—whether you are a company owner, a manager, a supervisor, or another kind of employee—you can use the techniques in this book to deal with all kinds of conflict between individuals and within groups.

This powerful, comprehensive method and the three-step model behind it are unique in that first they show you how to deal with the emotional fallout of conflict, and then they help you assess the contributing factors so that you can determine the best strategies for solution, by drawing on your faculties of reason and intuition. I call this approach the *Emotion-Reason-Intuition,* or ERI, model of resolving conflict, and I have been developing and refining it for more than a decade.

Use of the ERI model begins with steps that are intended to calm the *emotions* in the situation—your own or those of anyone else involved. Then you use *reason* to assess, understand, and evaluate the situation and the personalities caught up in it. (For example, instead of assuming that the problem is solved after you have cooled down an interpersonal flare-up, you may need to make a change in the organization itself: Does the interpersonal conflict have an underlying cause—perhaps a problem with the organization's structure, policies, or procedures?) Next, you use intuition to think of possible solutions and alternatives. Finally, you turn again to reason, in order to evaluate the possibilities for solution, and to intuition, in order to choose your eventual response to the difficult situation. Along the way, you use specific techniques for dealing with particular types of difficulties.

It may seem as if the ERI model calls for linear application of separate processes, but in reality its elements constitute a seamless, integrated whole whose elements you can draw on as you would draw on a repertoire of skills, using what is needed in particular situations. If you want to use the ERI model to solve an assortment of current problems, you will need to decide which problems should be addressed first. If there are just one or two, you can tackle them right away. When there are more, however, you will have to set priorities because you cannot deal effectively with more than one or two situations at a time.

To help you address and resolve difficult situations in your work environment, this book's introductory chapter (Chapter 1) presents an overview of the ERI model. The two chapters that follow in Part 1 discuss emotional barriers (Chapter 2) and communication problems (Chapter 3).

The four chapters in Part 2 help you use your reason to assess difficult situations. Chapter 4 shows you how to perceive organizational and political factors that may be contributing to difficulties, as well as how to recognize individual interests, wants, and needs and take them into account as you work toward your goals. Chapter 5 is a primer of sorts for working with difficult people. Chapter 6 shows you how to assess your characteristic style of handling conflict and, as necessary, choose others that are appropriate to various situations. Chapter 7 teaches you skills for negotiating.

The two chapters in Part 3 focus on using intuition, alone and in combination with reason. Chapter 8 helps you brainstorm alternatives for solving problems, and Chapter 9 shows you techniques for visualizing solutions.

Many experiences have contributed to the writing of this book. Chief among them has been my use of the Emotion-Reason-Intuition model in my own consulting work. I have made the ERI model available to hundreds of people in their attempts to solve workplace problems, and I can tell you that the model gets results. This book shows you how you can apply it in resolving your own workplace conflicts, whatever your position or type of organization.

ACKNOWLEDGMENTS

This book wouldn't have been possible without the input of the hundreds of people who shared their conflicts and how they worked on resolving them. Also, I gained insights from various programs I attended through many organizations that help in resolving conflicts, including Community Boards of San Francisco, the Society of Professionals in Dispute Resolution, the Northern California Council for Conflict Mediation, the Bay Area Organizational Development Network, and the Support Center for Nonprofit Management.

In addition, my special thanks to Community Boards of San Francisco, where I first learned about conflict resolution in the late 1980s when I participated as a volunteer panelist dealing with neighborhood disputes and went through a number of training programs to learn these skills.

ABOUT THE AUTHOR

Gini Graham Scott, Ph.D., J.D., is a nationally known writer, organizational and business consultant, speaker, and seminar/workshop leader whose specialties include organizational behavior, conflict resolution, creativity, problem solving, decision making, criminal justice, and social trends. She is founder and director of Changemakers and Creative Communications & Research.

Scott has taught at several business colleges, including the American Institute of Business and San Francisco College of Management. Classes include organizational behavior, marketing, psychological profiling, privacy, and ethics. She is the author of over thirty books including *Resolving Conflict with Others and Within Yourself, The Empowered Mind: How to Harness the Creative Force Within You, Mind Power: Picture Your Way to Success in Business, Building a Winning Sales Team,* and *Effective Selling and Sales Management.* In addition, she has developed a number of video scripts and training films in the areas of management and marketing and has written a dozen screenplays, drawing on her experience in criminal justice and legal issues.

She has also developed games and simulations that are used for training and development, and has had over two dozen games on the market with such major game companies as Hasbro Industries,

Pressman Toy, and Mag-Nif. She has published over three dozen songs as a songwriter and has written several dozen children's books.

Scott received her Ph.D. degree in sociology from the University of California, Berkeley, in 1976, her J.D. degree from the University of San Francisco Law School in 1990, and a Certificate in the Administration of Justice at Merritt College in 1999, and she is currently enrolled in an anthropology program at Merritt College, which she expects to lead to an M.A. degree.

She is active in a number of professional and business organizations, including the Oakland Chamber of Commerce, Bay Area Organizational Development Network, Bay Area Association for Psychological Type, American Society of Journalists and Authors, Authors Guild, and many others.

For more information, visit her web site at www.giniscott.com.

CHAPTER 1

Preparing to Work with Difficult Situations

Using the Emotion–Reason–Intuition, or ERI, model is a goal-oriented problem-solving process. At the very minimum, you can use the ERI model to shape your own behavior—and the more power and influence you have, the more you can accomplish, from working out a resolution with another party to finding a solution that affects a work team or the organization as a whole. Even in a situation where you can't work out an acceptable resolution, the ERI model can help you decide that the best option is to walk away—say, by taking a leave of absence, or even by leaving the organization—if you don't have the power to bring about changes in the behavior of other people. In most cases, however, the ERI model will help you find effective and creative alternatives for solving problems.

Situations involving workplace conflict can become especially tense and difficult to handle because walking away is often not an option: the conflict occurs between people who have to interact in ongoing relationships. Confusion can build, hostility can escalate, and other negative emotions can intensify. Meanwhile, in the early stages, the parties involved may want to ignore the problem in the hope that it will go away. And it may—until, as often happens, the hidden tension explodes into something worse.

Even a simple incident, as when one employee feels slighted when a co-worker doesn't show much interest in her new outfit, can escalate unexpectedly—say, if the seemingly uninterested employee is angry that this show-off colleague doesn't do enough serious work and so doesn't deserve any extra recognition. When two people have to continue working together, this type of feeling is often left unexpressed and may even be repressed; its existence is only hinted at by an unspoken chilliness that exists between the two, as in the following case.

Work Styles in Conflict

In a city prosecutor's office, an escalating conflict over radically different styles of work had brought Don and Julie, two assistant district attorneys, to the point of mutual hatred. Don was generally calm, laid back, and disorganized. His side of the office that he shared with Julie was piled high with files—a sign of his casual approach. He would often meet a friend for a long lunch and then work frantically to catch up. Julie, by contrast, was rigid, highly disciplined, controlling, and aggressive. She liked everything in its place, and so she kept her side of the office as neat as a pin and accomplished her work according to a weekly schedule. For several months the unexpressed tension between them had been growing. Because they worked independently, however, they said little to each other and steamed in silence.

Their conflict rapidly came to a boil when Lois, a student intern, came to work for both of them, and they discovered that they had very different ideas about what she should do and when she should do it. This discovery came about after Don put Lois to work on several of his cases and then left for a two-week vacation. With Don gone, Julie pulled Lois off Don's cases and put her to work on her own. Several days later, Don phoned in for a progress report on the work he had assigned to Lois. When she told him what Julie had done, he was furious.

Don returned from vacation, and Lois found herself caught in an acrimonious tug-of-war. Don and Julie took turns criticizing each other to her. The two of them griped and sniped for the two months that remained of Lois's internship, and the work of all three suffered from the high level of stress and tension. Don, feeling helpless to do anything about solving the problem, eventually requested and got a transfer to another department.

Holding down feelings to keep the focus on work does often maintain calm in the workplace and give antagonisms time to fade. When minor problems start to escalate, however, it's important to address the source of the problem. It's necessary to intervene, helping the individuals in conflict and the workplace as a whole promote both personal satisfaction and productivity. And occasionally, as in the case of Don and Julie, it may be best if someone leaves or a more systemic reorganization is done to eliminate the problem by changing the work environment—say, by reassigning the antagonists to different divisions, or at least to diffwerent work areas.

KNOWING WHEN TO USE THE ERI MODEL

The ERI model offers a clear lens through which to view difficult situations. Once you yourself have achieved the necessary calm detachment, you are more able to detect and cool down the emotions of others, analyze the problem, and assess what to do—drawing, as necessary, on your intuition in your efforts to help. The following three examples show managers and employees in various difficult situations to which the ERI model could be applied.

A Manager's Problem:
Two Employees' Personalities Clash

For Jim, supervisor of the sales division at a software design company, the conflict centered on a personality clash between two employees. They fought over job responsibilities, and Jim believed that they were trying to sabotage each other. One of them complained about missing phone messages and suspected the other of taking them; rumors were circulating about the other employee. Sometimes Jim felt an odd tension, as when he would pass a small group of employees having a conversation, and an uncomfortable silence would descend.

The antagonism between these two employees not only was affecting them, but it also was leading to delays and causing a decline in the sales division's productivity. Jim wasn't sure whether to discuss the problem with the whole department, talk individually with the two employees in turn, fire one of them, or wait and hope for the conflict to work itself out.

An Employee's Problem: Getting Too Personal

Judy was an administrative assistant in a small advertising agency. She liked her job and had developed a friendly relationship with her boss, Doris, an account executive. From time to time the two shared personal information and did small off-the-job favors for each other.

Judy's problem started when Doris went on maternity leave. Doris had already been out of the office for a few weeks when, ready to have her baby, she phoned Judy: her parents, she said, were in a nearby hotel; would Judy drive them to the hospital? Judy declined, explaining that she had another commitment.

After that, everything changed. When Doris returned to work, Judy noticed an unusual distance between them. She continued to do small favors for Doris, but Doris now said she was too busy to reciprocate in the old way. Doris also refused Judy's request to use an empty conference room for a meeting with two out-of-town friends during the lunch hour, a favor that Doris would have been quick to grant before.

Judy was disappointed that what had been a good relationship was suddenly different. She also felt some guilt over having turned Doris down, as well as resentment that Doris had expected her to do more than was possible. What was even more significant, though, is that Judy felt trapped: Doris was her boss and had the power to redefine their relationship.

Judy wondered what she should do. Say something? If so, what? Keep quiet and hope the problem would blow over? Quit before things got worse? Were there better alternatives?

Two Consultants in Conflict

Nancy, a management consultant, had problems with a fellow consultant, Joe, who had helped her establish her business and continued to give her advice as a mentor, as well as recommend clients to her. After Joe shared some personal information with Nancy, she mistakenly mentioned it to someone else, who then commented about it to Joe.

Joe was furious that Nancy had shared this information. He called her up, yelled at her, and then slammed down the receiver. When Nancy tried to call him back to apologize, Joe wouldn't take her call. When she wrote to explain how sorry she was, her letter came back marked "Return to sender." Nancy soon discovered that Joe was spreading stories about her, suggesting that she was incompetent in her work and that she had an intimate relationship with a client (an allegation that wasn't true).

Nancy was upset about her lost friendship with Joe as well as the lost business from referrals, and she felt guilty about causing the breach by her own indiscretion. But she was also hurt by Joe's slanderous remarks that could damage her business and wasn't sure what to do.

USING THE ERI MODEL TO MANAGE AND RESOLVE CONFLICT

The people in all three examples had two things in common: uncertainty about how to approach a work-related conflict, and negative feelings (anger, frustration, bitterness, guilt, confusion, resentment) that were a result of the conflict. Added to their negative feelings and uncertainty was the fear of making the wrong decision. How did the people in these examples use the ERI model?

A Manager Works Things Out

To solve the problem in his sales group, Jim turned to open communication, squarely facing the problem with the employees involved and then strategizing the best approach. He had no strong personal feelings about the problem, but he sensed that the two employees involved in the conflict did. Therefore, he focused on working with their emotions (the *E* phase of the ERI model). He took some time to determine whether the employees might benefit from expressing their feelings openly to each other, or whether they might prefer to express their feelings to him alone.

In order to make this determination, he talked with the employees separately, to let them know that he was aware of the conflict and to get a sense of their feelings. While talking with them, he evaluated the situation (the *R* phase of the ERI model) and considered alternatives (the *I* phase of the ERI model) in an effort to decide on the best approach (a combination of the *R* and *I* phases of the ERI model). Jim then let both employees know that he would tolerate no further actions on either one's part (actions such as not passing messages on and spreading rumors) that could sabotage the effectiveness of the sales group.

Jim monitored the situation for several days, to see if it would resolve itself. It did. The employee whose messages had been missing began to get them, and the rumors about the other employee stopped. Apparently Jim had made his point: they realized that their jobs were on the line now that Jim was aware of the situation.

Jim decided that he didn't need to bring the two employees together for a face-to-face confrontation, a meeting he felt it best to avoid, fearing that it could lead to an emotional explosion of charges and countercharges and make the working environment even more hostile. Instead, relying on indirection, he gave the two employees involved in the conflict an opportunity to express their feelings about each other in a safe, supportive environment: to him alone. (In many work situations, a more open discussion between the parties involved in a conflict might resolve deeper issues and result in a closer working relationship. In this case, the two employees worked in the same office but were not otherwise working together, and so Jim's more individualized approach was appropriate.)

Thereafter, the two employees were able to work effectively in the more neutral environment that Jim had created. Each of them also knew that further disruptions could mean dismissal. Over time, the rift between them healed, with neither one losing face.

An Employee Finds a Solution

Judy, the administrative assistant in the advertising agency, found a way to resolve the conflict in her too-personal relationship with Doris. First she got control of her anger toward Doris (the E phase) by recognizing that Doris was her boss and, as such, had more power in the relationship (the R phase). Then, as she looked more closely at the dynamics of the situation (R), she realized that her highest priority was keeping her job; therefore, she wanted to avoid an open confrontation with Doris. She also recognized that the primary source of the tension between herself and Doris was the imbalance entailed in the exchange of personal favors: because Doris had more power, Judy, by asking for favors, opened herself to the possibility that Doris might ask for disproportionately more in return.

Judy, combining reason and intuition (the I phase), realized that it would be best, if she wanted to keep her job, to let the situation cool down, be diplomatic and outwardly friendly, and continue working, as if nothing had happened. She also decided to pull back from her off-the-job friendship with Doris and to stop exchanging personal favors with her, thereby reducing the potential for conflict, since the exchange could never be equal.

As a result, Judy's relationship with Doris improved at work. With the elimination of off-the-job contact and conflict, a more neutral working environment was restored, one that was more comfortable for each of them.

A Consultant Applies the ERI Model

Nancy, by getting a grip on her own raging emotions (the E phase) and making a rational determination of what to do (the R and I phases), was able to resolve, at least for herself, what had become a very uncollegial relationship with a colleague. Her efforts to make direct contact with Joe had been rejected; therefore, she reasoned, Joe was probably still angry and hurt about what had happened.

Nancy concluded that she had two choices. One was to accept the split with Joe, overcome her own lingering feelings of hurt and anger, and, without taking legal action, counteract the rumors he had been spreading about her that were damaging her business. The other choice was to find a way of healing the rift and overcoming the bad feelings on both sides by using someone they both knew as a go-between, since Joe was refusing to have any direct contact with her; this mediator might be able to persuade Joe to listen to Nancy and accept her apology, and they might then be able to renew what had once been a good working relationship.

After much thought, Nancy chose the first alternative and left it up to Joe to initiate further contact with her: she felt that she had already made an honest effort to heal the breach, and that further efforts should be up to him. Accordingly, Nancy worked on healing her wounded feelings and overcoming any damaging remarks that might hurt her business. As a result, she finally gained a sense of release and improved her ability to compete for clients, while at the same time she remained receptive to the possibility of a future relationship with Joe.

As the three preceding examples illustrate, difficult situations can be handled quickly and effectively when the right approach is used. The "right" approach usually involves techniques for managing conflict by reducing or avoiding it, and conflict resolution can help the people involved to develop better relationships.

It is impossible to avoid conflict entirely, but there are three keys to resolving or minimizing conflict:

1. Recognize difficulties when they occur.

2. Decide when a problem is serious enough to warrant intervention.

3. Take action that is based on knowledge of what should be done to achieve the best result.

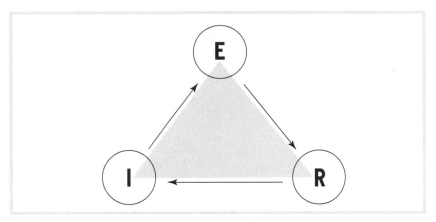

Figure 1 THE ERI MODEL

Doing this effectively involves getting emotional baggage out of the way, gaining insight into the factors contributing to the problem, and choosing wisely from a repertoire of possible responses—in other words, using the ERI model. You base your approach on the circumstances, personalities, interests, and needs of the people involved, as well as on your own goals, interests, and needs. The ERI model is presented schematically in Figure 1.

Each element of the model involves its own factors and strategies; as you work with the model, you will gain more expertise in using them. At first, you may have to consciously remind yourself to think about the various elements because they are unfamiliar. Gradually, however, as you continue to use this approach, the process will speed up and become second nature, so that you will think through problems very quickly and reach decisions in a flash. In fact, you will find that a kind of synergy occurs whereby you will simultaneously work with controlling emotion, using reason, and drawing on intuition to develop an optimal response to the particular circumstances. In effect, your intuition gives you the holistic picture of what to do, based on your understanding of the factors involved in the situation and on the repertoire of strategies you can use after the emotions have been brought under control. By the same token, it may be possible to isolate the specific factors contributing to a conflict, as well as the strategies to use in resolving it. Nevertheless, in practice everything comes together: the strategies you use are closely integrated with the contributing factors that you identify. The ERI model works because it helps you look at any conflict in two ways:

1. It provides a broad *general* framework for analyzing the contributing elements and for using this understanding to make a strategic assessment of techniques for resolution.

2. It provides a three-step method for addressing any *particular* conflict.

An enhanced schema of the ERI model, with the specific factors and strategies added for each element, is shown in Figure 2.

QUESTIONS AND CRITERIA FOR USING THE ERI MODEL

The basic way to use the ERI model is to regard each conflict or difficult situation less as a conflict or difficulty per se than as a problem to be solved. Begin by asking yourself the following questions:

- What is the nature of the problem?

- What do I want? What do others want?

- What do we need?

- How important is it to solve this problem?

- What solution(s) would I prefer? What solution(s) would others prefer?

- How many ways are there for implementing the possible solution(s)? What are the best ways?

Your success in making choices about solutions will depend on how successfully you can take the following steps:

- Control, defuse, or eliminate the negative emotional environment that is contributing to the problem and blocking its solution.

- Make a rational assessment of the available alternatives.

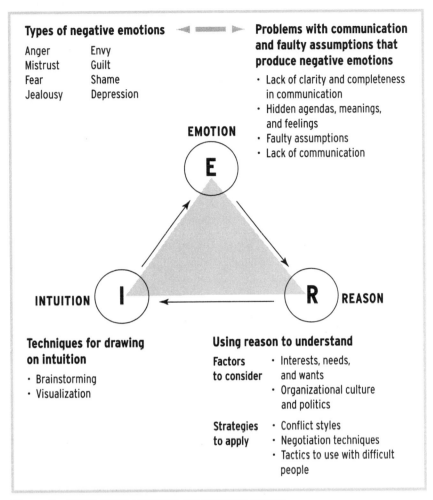

Figure 2 ENHANCED SCHEMA OF THE ERI MODEL

- Intuitively determine your best choices for dealing with the situation.

The rest of this book focuses on helping you make these choices effectively by showing you how to work with the elements of the ERI model.

PART 1

WORKING WITH EMOTION

Negative emotions—anger, mistrust, fear, jealousy, envy, guilt, shame—contribute to problems and stand in the way of solutions. They are like a wall of fire: the intense heat of these emotions pushes people apart, and the emotional "smoke" of the conflagration prevents clear vision. Thus these emotions fuel misunderstandings, false assumptions, communication difficulties, and the other factors that lead to problems, but they also act as barriers to understanding and reconciliation.

As we have seen, using the ERI model means first gaining control of emotions and overcoming emotional barriers to conflict resolution. As part of this process, it is necessary to clear up the communication problems that often trigger negative emotional responses or result from them. The two chapters in Part 1 discuss these two topics: overcoming emotional barriers (Chapter 2) and clearing up miscommunications (Chapter 3).

CHAPTER 2

Overcoming Emotional Barriers to Conflict Resolution

One of the biggest barriers to resolving any conflict is the emotional baggage that gets in the way—feelings like anger, mistrust, jealousy, depression, and fear. Such feelings may often be expressed openly, as when someone erupts with hostility or retreats in fear. At other times, feelings like these simmer just under the surface and lead to behind-the-scenes backstabbing, sabotage, and elaborate schemes for revenge.

Sometimes, however, emotional barriers take the form of deeply hidden invaders. In these cases, the person involved in a conflict harbors negative feelings but is not consciously aware of them, although they color his or her actions and reactions. If another party to the conflict is similarly acting out hidden feelings, then the problem can become even worse: both sides are fighting blind, propelled by profoundly unconscious negative forces that cannot be controlled, simply because they are unconscious.

As we have seen in our discussion of the Emotion-Reason-Intuition (ERI) model, no difficult situation can be successfully resolved while emotions are putting up an obstacle. Therefore, this chapter focuses on getting feelings out of the way in order to clear the path for understanding and constructive action.

UNCONSCIOUS EMOTIONS

The following example illustrates how unrecognized negative feelings can exacerbate a problem and undermine one's ability to resolve it successfully.

Repressed Resentment Leads to Unconscious Sabotage

Belinda worked in the research division of a company that manufactured products from recycled materials. Her job was to provide information to people in various departments, and she generally did so as quickly as she could, eager to help. Her company stressed a philosophy of service to both customers and members of the organization, and Belinda was committed to that ideal herself.

But then she received a series of requests for research assistance from Cynthia in another department of the company. At first there were just a few requests and Belinda was happy to comply. But gradually the number of requests mounted, and Belinda began to resent all the extra work. However, she felt uncomfortable admitting her irritation even to herself because of the company's policy. In addition, she liked seeing herself as a helpful, cooperative person. So instead of facing her true feelings, she began to find excuses for why she couldn't finish the work for Cynthia. These excuses were not just for Cynthia; Belinda unconsciously created them for herself. For example, once or twice she mislaid Cynthia's assignment. Sometimes she couldn't find the research source material Cynthia needed. At other times she made mistakes in giving research results to Cynthia, so that Cynthia would be embarrassed when she cited incorrect data in a company report; then if Cynthia complained, Belinda would have the correct data on hand, making it seem that Cynthia had made the mistake herself.

Belinda was unconsciously undermining the value of the work she did for Cynthia because she felt that Cynthia was exploiting her. Not only was Cynthia asking her to do additional work, but she was not showing her any special appreciation by acknowledging her help. Belinda repressed her feelings because she was convinced she shouldn't feel this way. Her unacknowledged resentment found an outlet in her efforts to counter the help she didn't want to give. In time, Cynthia reacted by angrily confronting Belinda, while Belinda innocently stonewalled, claiming that she was doing the best she could in the face of many dead-lines from other people.

This situation could only get worse, eventually erupting into a more serious confrontation, a decline in workplace productivity, and other problems, unless Belinda realized what she was doing and the negative behavior stopped or a manager intervened to find a solution.

How do you know when you're harboring unconscious emotional barriers? After all, they are by definition out of your awareness. In fact, they may be hidden because you don't want to recognize or acknowledge anger, hostility, depression, or similarly destructive, negative feelings. How can you bring unconscious feelings into your awareness so you can work with them, much as you already work with all the feelings of which you are aware?

1. *Notice when you have inexplicably strong, unusual, disproportionate reactions to someone or to some event.* Such reactions can point to unconscious influences or motives. Regard them as signals that something is wrong. They suggest a disconnection between your behavior (presumably motivated by reason) and your unconscious feelings (which are out of sync with your behavior).

2. *Explore your feelings, and try to discover why you feel the way you do.* If you can learn to do this, you will have a skill to which you can turn whenever you need to work with hidden feelings. Start by going to a quiet place and letting yourself enter a quiet, relaxed state. Do whatever you must to put yourself into this state: turn down the lights, close your eyes, and so on. Then, when you are completely relaxed, ask yourself some questions about the difficult situation and your reactions to it:

   • Is there something about this situation that is making me uncomfortable?

   • How do I really feel about the other people involved in it?

   • What names do I have for how I feel? Am I feeling anger? hostility? resentment? fear? Is anything in this situation provoking these feelings?

• How intense are my feelings? What is their importance to me? Can I set them aside? Or should I let them guide me in deciding what to do?

Don't try to answer these questions logically; just let the answers come to you in your relaxed, meditative state. Maybe the answers will come as images seen by your mind's eye, as on a screen. Perhaps they will come as messages delivered by an inner voice. Use a notebook to write down what you are seeing or hearing, either as the experience is occurring or later on, or speak into a tape recorder. The point is to try to dredge up from your unconscious a clearer picture of what you are feeling and why, so you can then use this knowledge to decide how to control and best deal with these feelings.

3. *Ask someone else to help you uncover your feelings.* Because it can be very difficult to discover on your own what's really wrong, it may be helpful to seek help from someone else: a close friend, a relative, a clergyman, or a professional counselor. In some cases, a trusted work associate or colleague can be of help, but be careful: it is important not to poison the relationships that your associates and colleagues have with a party involved in a conflict with you, nor is it wise to risk undermining your relationships with your associates and colleagues by appearing to seem less than competent, professional, and in control of yourself. Therefore, when you need help uncovering your hidden feelings, it may be best to ask for help from people who have no personal or collegial ties to anyone with whom you are having a difficulty.

CONSCIOUS EMOTIONS

Most of the time in situations of conflict, the problem is that feelings are close to the surface, even openly expressed, and their expression is blocking the resolution of the conflict. Further, the more the feelings intensify and are expressed in action (as in the case of mounting anger or mistrust), the more they get in the way. For example, a conflict can begin with a simple difference of opinion about how to organize a project, but as the debate intensifies and tempers flare, hostility escalates until the conflict is now more about personalities than about the original issue. Mistrust also intensifies in such situations and undermines the ability of people to work together. To a certain extent, expressing feelings is like letting off excess steam in a kettle. But if there is no way for the released steam to dissipate, it soon fills up the room. Therefore, it is crucial to be sensitive and know how to control, direct, deflect, or otherwise handle strong feelings, whether they're your own or someone else's.

Putting a Damper on Rage

Joslyn worked as public relations assistant to Allison, a poor communicator, in a company where all policies and procedures were subject to the approval of the CEO—and he had been known to change his mind well into a project, creating extra work and pressure for everyone else. But Joslyn appreciated her job security, and she liked her co-workers. In fact, the pressure and chaos under which they all worked had forged a strong camaraderie. One day, though, it all felt like too much for Joslyn. She wanted to explode.

Allison had asked her to organize a big event to announce a new product line. A key part of this effort had involved preparing a press release several weeks before the event and contacting the media. Normally a product rollout would be covered in the business pages of the newspaper, if at all. But Joslyn, to ensure a good turnout, planned to notify a variety of community and hobbyist groups as well. Thus, when reporters arrived to cover the event, it would have the atmosphere of a community fair. Joslyn even arranged for some high-level community leaders to attend: their presence would help further the company's image as a contributor to the community.

After Josyln had prepared all the publicity releases and phoned leaders in many of the community and hobbyist groups, she was unable to follow through, because she had encountered an unexpected obstacle: Allison.

Allison, busy with another project, was frequently away from the office. When Joslyn tried to get final approval of her plans and coordinate her efforts with Allison's, Allison was too rushed to talk, and she didn't return Joslyn's calls.

Joslyn, blocked and stymied, was not even sure that the event was going forward. Had the CEO changed his mind, as he had done so often before? None of Allison's colleagues seemed to know. "Ask Allison," they said.

After two weeks of this treatment, Joslyn began to feel insulted and angry, but she continued to focus on doing what she could to organize an event that might or might not occur. And she finally did get Allison's okay—a week before the event, in passing, as Allison breezed by Joslyn's desk. There now remained only a few days in which to make the event a success. To make matters worse, Joslyn felt that she would be the one held responsible if the event turned out to be a failure. That was when she reached the explosion point.

Joslyn wanted to tell Allison just what she thought of her. She felt ready to walk off the job. She was prepared to tell Allison that the event just could not go forward—and, even more, that she was frustrated by this typically chaotic pattern of behavior on Allison's part. She got up and started toward Allison's office—and then she caught herself.

She managed to calm herself, and then she went to a trusted co-worker, who listened to her and agreed with Joslyn about why she was feeling so angry. Then, along with a few other co-workers, he pitched in to help Joslyn do the follow-through work for the planned event.

Joslyn now understood that she would be better off working somewhere else, but she also realized that expressing her anger openly would be a losing effort, since Allison was her supervisor and had all the power. Moreover, she was able to see that Allison's style was merely a reflection of the company's culture, as embodied by the CEO.

WORKING WITH SPECIFIC EMOTIONS

The three common manifestations of negative emotion are anger, mistrust, and fear.

Anger

If you're angry, it's usually best to bring your anger under control, either so you don't express it directly or, in certain situations, so you can strategically express it in a controlled, measured way, letting others know that you are seriously upset and are motivated to take effective action. The main differential in whether to hold back or express anger in a controlled way is power: if you have less power than others involved in the conflict, then it is best not to show your anger, since you don't control the outcome, and any display of anger will generally weaken your position. Conversely, if you have more power, a controlled show of anger may help motivate others to behave as you want them to behave (for example, a tardy, forgetful employee may be prompted to pay more attention and be on time). When parties to a conflict have equal power, it is usually best to hold back, although a strategic display of anger may be effective at times. In any case, the goal is to become like an actor, in charge of your emotions and able to express them or not.

There are some specific techniques for controlling anger:

- *Use a personal cue that reminds you to control your anger.* For example, when anger starts to mount, press your fingers together as a signal to pay attention and put on the brakes, or count to ten, or tap your wrist. Take some time to practice the association between your chosen cue and the relaxation response that you want, so that relaxation becomes a conditioned reflex. Then, when you use your cue in a difficult situation, it works on an unconscious level to tell you to relax.

- *Use self-talk to tell yourself you need to control your anger and calm down.* For example, repeat to yourself a few words like "Calm down, calm down," or "Don't show you're mad, don't show you're mad." You can do this even in the heat of a difficult situation, while you are feeling a surge of anger.

- *Take a time-out.* Then you can quietly unwind and talk to yourself, or you can punch a pillow to release your feelings. Do whatever you have to in order to regain control. Diplomatically excuse yourself, if you need to, or delay discussion with the other party while you calm down. Then, when you're ready, return to address the problem, and seek to resolve it. If the problem is serious enough and recurs often enough, eventually it may be best for you to remove yourself; the job may not be sufficient compensation for the continuing emotional upset. Here, too, if this is your decision, it's best not to make it in the heat of the moment,

How Do You Know When It's Time to Go?

When it's time to take permanent leave of a situation, how will you know? This radical action may be warranted when the following conditions exist:

- The build-up of anger and hostility is very great and seems likely to increase.

- Previous efforts to solve the problem haven't worked, and the realistic prospects for its future solution look dim.

- You feel increasingly drained by your anger and frustration over not having been able to solve the problem to your satisfaction.

- You find yourself spending too much time dealing with the situation and its emotional fallout.

- You want to move on and make a fresh start.

If you're leaning toward getting out of the situation altogether, first take these steps:

- Do a cost-benefit analysis: Would the losses of staying in the situation be greater than the losses of leaving? Would the gains of staying be fewer than the gains of leaving?

- Reassure yourself that it's all right to cut your losses. Give yourself permission to let go and move on.

Once you've actually decided to leave, it may be helpful to take the following steps:

- As necessary, keep telling yourself that you've made the right decision and that it's time to move on.

- Look ahead with confidence to the future, examining the painful past only in order to learn from it.

- Move on. Let yourself feel good that you're getting out. Tell yourself you're ready to do whatever comes next.

when you are in the grip of emotional turmoil. First calm your-self, and then, if you must, take a permanent time-out. (See "How Do You Know When It's Time to Go?" on p. 22 for guid-ance about knowing when to take this more radical step.)

- *Find something positive that you like to do.* For example, hit a ball on the golf course or on the tennis court. Go for a swim or a workout in the gym. Go to a party, or go shopping with friends. See a movie, or get a massage. Direct your attention to this activ-ity while your anger dissipates. When you hold back your feelings in one situation, the inhibited emotional charge may be set off in another situation that has nothing to do with the first one. An activity that you enjoy can help dissipate these feelings in a harmless and even productive way.

Mistrust

Another barrier to good working relationships, and a key factor in their breakdown, is lack of trust. Conflicts due to mistrust can occur when someone isn't completely forthright, gives out misleading information, suggests he knows something when he doesn't, omits details in order to cover up mistakes, or lies outright.

What can be done? If the person caught in a lie is one's subordi-nate, the solution may be to put him on notice and fire him if he lies again (unless his work is so valuable that the mistrust he inspires can be overlooked). But what if he is your co-worker or your boss? Then the issue can be more complicated, and you have to weigh your mis-trustful feelings against the benefits of the relationship.

Trusting Feelings
of Mistrust

Fred owned and operated a small company that provided service workers to homeowners. Fred's employees offered skills ranging from gardening to household repair, and Andy was one of the best—at least when he showed up.

The trouble was, Andy was always having problems at home: a death in the family, a sick son, a daughter in conflict with her preschool teacher, tenants in his house who needed help moving, and so on. Over and over, Fred tried to be supportive and under-standing, and over and over Andy agreed to go out on jobs but then showed up late, if he got there at all. Later, Andy would offer Fred a good excuse, tell Fred the problem was under control, and then go off and do his usual good job. More and more, however, Andy's behavior was producing a domino effect as delays caused by his behavior were aggravated by uncontrollable factors like the weather, with the result that work had to be rescheduled.

Instead of confronting Andy directly, Fred continued to accept Andy's explanations. He didn't want to suggest that Andy's fam-ily problems were unimportant, but he had growing doubts about Andy's priorities. He also hesitated to replace Andy, because he valued Andy's wide variety of skills. As a result, he often found himself making excuses to customers to explain delays. Meanwhile, his mistrust of Andy was beginning to invade areas in which Andy was in fact being completely honest with him. For instance, Fred began to doubt Andy's estimates of hours on the job, the costs that Andy reported for replacement parts, and the accuracy of Andy's accounts of time spent. Whenever Fred checked out the figures they were correct, but his doubts remained.

Finally, after a whole week in which Andy didn't return his calls, Fred decided it was time to move on. This time when Andy showed up with his usual string of excuses, Fred was psycholog-ically prepared to let him go. He told Andy that their working relationship had to end: he could no longer trust Andy, and he no longer wanted to go on trying. When he finally trusted his feel-ings of mistrust, he was able to take this step, and he felt a great sense of relief.

In contrast to Fred's continual delays and discomfort with con-fronting Andy, one of the first steps to take in dealing with feelings of mistrust is to bring them to the surface. Fred didn't do that with Andy; as a result, he eventually had no alternative but to let a skilled employee go.

Trust is the glue that keeps working relationships together. If you aren't sure whether to trust someone, you may act very uncertainly with her—holding back information, for example, or hesitating before fully committing yourself to work on a project with her. Mistrust may not work its destruction right away, but over time it may cause the complete breakdown of a good working relationship. And when feelings of mistrust are themselves mistrusted, this secondary mistrust can prolong a relationship that really should end.

Getting feelings of mistrust out in the open, and sooner rather than later, also gives you a way to determine whether the mistrust is justified. It's generally best to raise your concerns directly with the person you mistrust and try to clear the air that way. Indirect ways of airing your suspicions (such as talking too freely with a group of other co-workers) may serve only to complicate the relationship still further.

If you find that there is an objective basis for your mistrustful feelings, you can make an informed decision. You may choose to exercise more caution in the relationship, or you may opt not to continue the relationship at all. In short, there are several steps to be taken when you are dealing with feelings of mistrust in a working relationship:

- Confront the situation directly, and press for resolution so that you and the other person can work together in a spirit of trust in the future.

- If you feel you can't raise the issue directly because the risk is too great (for example, you risk losing your job before you are ready to quit), you can take steps to protect yourself in your future dealings with the other person. You can become more distant, delay working with him or her, or otherwise take a cautious, test-the-waters approach.

- You can walk away from the situation and move on. If this is your choice, try to leave diplomatically, without turning your departure into a confrontation that causes defensiveness, hard feelings, and, perhaps, problems for you down the line. Leaving diplomatically also lets you walk into the future without the burden of emotional baggage from the past.

Fear

When you're afraid that something may or may not happen in a working relationship with someone, you should handle your fear much as you would handle feelings of mistrust. The first step is to share your concerns with the other person, when it's possible to do so, and determine whether your fear is justified. That way, you can handle the problem openly instead of proceeding on the basis of false perceptions or faulty assumptions. If your fear is one that others share but haven't expressed, your bringing your own fear into the open can help all of you deal with it as a group.

Some fears are phantom fears—for example, in a work group, fear fueled by false rumors of impending layoffs. This kind of fear can affect morale and lead valued employees to start looking for new jobs; bringing it into the open can reassure people and stop the proliferation of rumors. Other fears are very real, but in these cases the fear can be addressed, and a decision can be made about how to handle it. For example, if you are afraid of giving an upcoming presentation because it may not be good enough to satisfy your boss, you may be able to overcome your fear by practicing your presentation. It may even help you to share your fear with your boss, if she is receptive, so that she can help you do better—say, by offering you training, or by pairing you with a more experienced employee as a mentor your first time out. Not only will you feel less fear; you also will have taken steps to make sure that your presentation goes well.

TOOLS FOR MANAGING EMOTIONS

The key to working with negative emotions—whether anger, fear, or mistrust, and whether they are your own emotions or someone else's—is to find a way for them to be confronted and controlled so that they can be expressed, released, or redirected in positive, productive ways. This is especially important if you are in a low-power position, where unseemly or untimely displays of emotion can elicit a range of negative reactions from higher-ups—dismissal, demotion, loss of privileges or pay, or some combination of these measures. Even if you are in a high-power position, expressing negative emotions too often, too intensely, or at the wrong times can bring consequences: a decline in employees' morale, their hesitation to take leadership roles or reveal important but negative information, a trench-warfare mentality among employees, resulting in a decline in cooperation and teamwork.

Working with Your Own Emotions

As we have seen, it's important that you take charge of your negative emotions when they arise so that you can avoid acting inappropriately or rashly in the heat of the moment. But it's also important that you pay attention to what these emotions are telling you.

Listen to your negative emotions. They are an early warning of something wrong—a problem, or an imbalance that needs to be corrected. For example, if you as a supervisor feel fearful before or during a meeting that otherwise seems routine, your feelings may be a signal of some unexpressed problem in the company—perhaps mounting tension in your work group, which no one wants to talk about. Although it may not be wise to mention your feelings at the meeting itself, afterward you can examine your fears more coolly and decide how to proceed. Similarly, you may often feel angry or mistrustful about the way someone is behaving: you suspect a hidden agenda at odds with the company's or your own, you sense that the other person doesn't like you, or you feel a knot in your stomach when you are around this person. For the moment, it's best to hold back on expressing your feelings. Then, after you have calmed yourself, you can determine whether your feelings are justified—by exploring your feelings alone or with a helper, confiding discreetly in others, or perhaps keeping a log of your anger or of events that support your suspicions. At that point, you can decide what would be the best thing to do: continue to control your feelings? exercise greater caution around this person? talk with the person about his or her behavior? find a temporary or permanent way out of the situation? Worksheet 1 can help you assess your own negative emotions in such a situation and decide how you want to approach its resolution.

Working with Others' Emotions

When another person is noticeably experiencing negative feelings (usually anger or fear), you can help this person manage and control his or her emotions to aid in resolving whatever situation is provoking these feelings. If you are directly involved in the situation, you will often have to get control of your own emotions first.

Once you have your feelings in check, choose an approach that feels comfortable to you. The specific one you choose will depend on

WORKSHEET 1

Assessing the Barriers Presented by My Emotions

What is the problem or conflict I am experiencing?

_____

_____

_____

What kinds of negative emotions am I feeling? What can I do to control or deal with these emotions?

_____

_____

_____

Why do I feel this way? What evidence is there to support my feelings?

_____

_____

_____

How can I express or control my feelings? (List all the possibilities you can think of, and then set realistic priorities for what you can and would like to do.)

_____

_____

_____

_____

_____

_____

_____

_____

_____

_____

your own style of dealing with conflict (more about this in Chapter 6) and your assessment of the other person's conflict style. The suggestions that follow can be useful regardless of whether you and the other person have equal power in your working relationship.

1. *Suggest a cooling-off period.* This will give both of you a chance to calm down. (Even if you already have your own emotions in check, it can help to suggest this time-out for both of you, so the other person won't feel defensive about his or her own emotional reactions.) You can then meet again to discuss the problem—maybe in an hour, maybe the next day. The cooling-off period can also be used to gather facts about the situation so that you can both discuss it more rationally—such as when you are both upset by a project meltdown and are blaming each other.

2. *Listen to the other person's anger, fears, or other concerns.* In some cases, instead of taking a time-out, it may be better just to let the other person vent. (Again, listening can be helpful even if you already have your own emotions in check—and even if you don't, you can bring your own feelings under control while you listen.) Listening is an especially good approach under the following conditions:

   • When the other person's feelings are so intense that waiting is not an option

   • When the other person isn't willing to listen to you

   • When the other person's hostility or suspicion is blocking communication to such an extent that a cooling-off period would not be helpful

   Remember, listening without responding doesn't mean that you agree with what is being said. Don't argue, don't defend, don't express judgments, and—to the extent possible—don't even entertain judgments. Rather, show that you want to understand. Listen to the other person's information, and listen for unspoken information. This approach is sometimes called *active listening*. (See "Keys to Good Listening," in Chapter 3, for guidance on using the active listening technique.) Worksheet 2, on page 30, can help you assess the barriers presented by others' negative emotions in such a situation and decide how to approach resolution.

WORKSHEET 2

Assessing the Barriers Presented by Others' Emotions

What problem or conflict is leading _____ to have negative feelings?

_____

_____

_____

What kinds of negative emotions does _____ appear to be feeling?

_____

_____

_____

Why might _____ feel this way? What might I have done to contribute to these feelings?

_____

_____

_____

How can I help _____ control or deal with these feelings? (List all the possibilities you can think of, and then set priorities for what you can and would like to do.)

_____

_____

_____

_____

_____

_____

_____

_____

_____

_____

CHAPTER 3

Clearing Up
Communication Problems

Good communication can solve some problems, but poor communication can be the cause of many more. Typical everyday breakdowns in communication can occur when one person isn't clear or another doesn't listen, or when one party says and means one thing and a listener thinks he said or meant something else. Sometimes there is no communication at all, or there is too little, with confusion, anger, and frustration as the result. At other times there is too much communication, as when someone reveals a message that was communicated in confidence or violates an agreement about privacy.

The list of possible problems is almost endless, and any of them may arise from or lead to negative emotional states (anger, resentment, jealousy, fear, and so on). These negative emotions in turn may cause further breakdowns in communication, until interactions between people become a downward spiral in which communication and negative emotions feed each other, making problems worse and perhaps even undermining a whole organization, as in the following example.

Poor Communication Destroys
a Nonprofit Agency

Community Aid was a nonprofit organization that arranged for teams of volunteers to participate in a variety of public service activities. Each volunteer team had its own board of directors, and each board had the authority to make decisions about its own team's programs. There was also an organization-level staff coordinator, who had two principal duties: helping each of the boards carry out its programs, and presenting proposed programs to the organization's general board in order to verify that the programs would be in keeping with the overall mission and policies of the larger organization. Again, however, apart from the need for this verification, each board was empowered to act autonomously.

Jane, the staff coordinator for Community Aid, had a problematic style of communication. At meetings of the individual boards, for example, she often failed to provide complete information about the larger organization's policies and resource limitations. As a result, board members would plan programs, only to discover later on that the programs were unrealistic—there wasn't enough money or staff support to carry them out. Jane also had the habit of communicating team-level board decisions to the general board but then waiting several months to tell board members whether the proposed programs were feasible. The delays left board members frustrated because they were unable to move ahead with their plans. Some board members also suspected Jane of hiding behind supposed organizational limitations as a way of thwarting programs that she personally didn't want to see go forward.

The predictable result was frequent conflict. One board president resigned in a huff because he felt unable to get anything accomplished. Another volunteer, who was trying to organize a program to decorate a community room for homeless people, blew up at a board meeting when Jane announced that there would be another month's delay while she spoke to the general board about this program to "make sure that everyone approved." "But it's not their decision!" the volunteer shouted. "Our board is supposed to make these decisions."

Leaders of the team-level boards eventually had a discussion with Jane about this communication pattern, and Jane agreed to confine herself to the scope of her job description: helping board members carry out their plans (rather than making covert decisions herself), and being more forthcoming with the necessary information. A few weeks later, however, it was again business as usual: little or no information from Jane.

Over the next few months, most of the board leaders, seeing that Jane was unlikely to change, backed off from taking the initiative, and some even left their teams. Meanwhile, as teams with fewer leaders organized fewer programs, many more volunteers drifted away. With its teams leaderless, dispirited, and in disarray, Community Aid became increasingly ineffective as an organization.

BASIC PRINCIPLES OF GOOD COMMUNICATION

The basic principles of good communication may sound like little more than common sense: be clear, be direct, be complete, and be appropriate. Nevertheless, many people are unaware of these principles, or they fail to observe them. As you read this chapter, try noticing how different people communicate in your own workplace or in other areas of your life. Notice the way that clear, direct, complete, appropriate communication contributes to good relationships and improved productivity, whatever the goal, whereas unclear, indirect, incomplete, inappropriate communication undermines relationships and group activity. Then, when you notice a problem in communication at work, think about how changes might be made to improve the situation. Unless you are in a position to implement organizational changes, it may be best at this stage to keep your observations and proposed solutions to yourself; just be attentive as a way of promoting your own awareness of communication and your ability to make changes wherever you can. You can use Worksheet 3, on page 34, to help you do this.

Problems Related to Clarity and Completeness

When communications are unclear or incomplete, people are uncertain about what to do. In this situation, people may do the wrong things, or the wrong people may take action.

Sometimes people who offer unclear or incomplete communications do so because they are uncertain themselves. It would be better if they could ask for clarification or more information, or if they simply disclosed their lack of clarity and information. Then everyone involved would have a better understanding of the situation, and people could work together rather than at cross-purposes. Another

WORKSHEET 3

Noticing Communication Problems at Work

Individuals in the Organization	Communication Problems		Ways to Improve Communication	
	With Me	With Others	By Me	By Others

reason someone may offer unclear or incomplete communication is discomfort with the topic of the message: perhaps it involves embarrassing, unpleasant, or otherwise negative information. Then, too, there may be scheduling pressures, so that the person wants to spend as little time as necessary giving details. It's also possible that offering incomplete information is a way of avoiding responsibility by talking around the matter at hand (and secretly hoping, meanwhile, that it will go away).

The problem is not always entirely with the speaker, however. Sometimes the listener can contribute to the problem by not acknowledging his own lack of clarity, uncertainty, or confusion. Perhaps he is embarrassed to admit his ignorance, or he feels that his supervisor doesn't have the time, patience, or understanding to fill him in. And sometimes the listener is unaware of how much clarity he really lacks.

Whatever the causes, when poor communication is combined with poor listening, the result is miscommunication and, often, a vicious circle of further miscommunication, as in the following examples:

- A boss doesn't give clear instructions and then is unhappy when the employee makes an inevitable mistake.

- An employee doesn't understand what she is asked to do but then tries to figure out for herself what to do and gets it wrong.

- The company official gives an independent contractor unclear specifications for a product and then is not only embarrassed but out a great deal of money when the contractor brings back the wrong product.

Breakdowns of this kind are represented in Chart 1.

When unclear or incomplete communication creates a problem, the solution is usually obvious: if you don't fully understand something, or if you think someone else doesn't fully understand, then take steps to make the communication clear and complete. If you are the person in charge, you should also take whatever steps are necessary to change the working environment itself so that it encourages and supports clear and complete communication. Here are some other ways to ensure that communication is clear and complete:

CHART 1	
Communication Breakdown	
Communication by the Speaker	**Response of the Listener**

Nature of the Failure	
Lack of clarity	Failure to ask for clarity
Lack of completeness	Failure to ask for more information
Reason for the Failure	
Lack of information	Unawareness of a lack of clarity
Uncertainty of the speaker	Uncertainty about the message
Discomfort of the speaker	Uncertainty about the message and the reasons for any discomfort
Possible Emotional Response	
Anger	Anger
Frustration	Frustration
Distrust	Distrust

- Document your verbal messages with written follow-up memos, and then follow up on those memos to make sure that they were read and understood.

- If you hear or read something from someone and aren't sure what the person has said, wants, or means, then ask the person to clarify, or ask someone else who understands this information to explain. Don't let embarrassment stop you from admitting you don't know something; you will only make things worse if you act on the basis of incomplete information, since mistakes will be more likely.

- To check your understanding, repeat what you think the other person has said. This kind of checking can also help to show the other person that you are listening and interested. Don't overdo this, of course; you don't want to seem dense or bog the conversation down. Performing this exercise from time to time, however, serves as a useful reality check and gets you and the other party on the "same page."

- If you are the one who is communicating information, do your own check from time to time to make sure that what you are saying has been correctly received and understood. For example, ask the other person to tell you what he or she understands your message to be. It can be especially helpful to do this when you are giving very important, complex, or timely information.

- When you are giving information, look for signs that the other person understands (or doesn't), and respond accordingly.

- If you discover that information you have given has been misunderstood, take some time to go into more detail, to clarify or expand on what you said before, and make sure this time that the information really is understood.

- If others seem to find your information hard to understand, simplify it or break it up into smaller, easier-to-receive pieces.

- If the person with whom you are talking seems misinformed, correct the misinformation without making the other person uncomfortable about hearing the correction. As an employer, for example, correct without blame or shame. As an employee, diplomatically suggest your correction so that your emloyer will be more receptive to accepting it.

- If you are working in a group and some members seem to be getting unclear or incomplete information, ask all the participants to check with one another to make sure that everyone has the same understanding of the information, and correct any misunderstandings. This kind of check can be carried out in a particular situation or, if misunderstanding is a systemic problem in your group, conduct such checks on a continuing basis.

Problems Related to Noncommunication

When someone doesn't communicate enough, you don't know what is going on, and you don't have the important information you need—or maybe you don't even know what information you need. The solution to such a problem seems obvious: you can ask for the information you need, or you can ask the person to give you more information on a regular basis; and, if your position is equal or superior to that of the person from whom you want more information, it will certainly be easier for you to ask. Thus, for instance, you can ask your co-worker to keep you advised of progress on a project, and perhaps even to copy you on memos, or you can ask someone you supervise to keep you informed, via follow-up reports on meetings or copies of letters and memos, about what he or she is doing to carry out an assigned task.

But what if the poor communicator is your supervisor? Now the situation is more difficult because a superior may see an attempt to discuss a communication problem as an attack on his or her authority, or as a criticism of his or her abilities as a supervisor. If the problem is serious enough to affect your productivity or your desire to stay in the job, then it's worth pursuing if you prefer to stay. Just find a way to be tactful and diplomatic in the way you discuss the matter. Suggest rather than confront. Perhaps put your comments in a memo that emphasizes how things could be improved rather than why things are going wrong. Raise the issue only with your supervisor at first, not with his or her superiors, so that he or she will be better able to listen or make changes without losing face.

The way to deal with a problem of no communication, or too little communication, will vary greatly according to the circumstances, the differences in power between the individuals involved, and other factors. In general, however, the key to resolving a no-communication problem is, not unexpectedly, communication. To the extent that you can, be open. Talk about whatever is uncertain or unclear. Explain what you need to know to do your job more effectively, and tactfully urge the other person to be more forthcoming for your mutual benefit.

If you are the one responsible for communicating information, consider whether your message has reached everyone who needs to hear it. Has anyone been left out? And is the information complete enough for others to fully understand, or do you need to provide more details? Does anyone seem confused or uncertain? If so, he or she may need more information, or more information of a particular kind, as may people who are making mistakes.

Also ask yourself what will be the best way for the information in question to be given and received: by way of a phone call? a personal meeting? a written message or memo? a notice posted on a bulletin board? Some combination of these methods may be needed, as may repetition and follow-up. And, given today's information glut and the myriad competing messages we all receive, it is generally better, when a message is important, to err on the side of offering too much information and follow-up. Worksheet 4 can help you fully communicate necessary information in various forms to all the people who need to know.

HIDDEN AGENDAS, MEANINGS, AND FEELINGS

A person hears or interprets a message according to his or her own agenda. There is a discrepancy between what a person says and the person's body language—between the verbal content and the nonverbal body language that comes across. Someone says something, but underneath the message is a concealed purpose or unspoken feeling. These are instances of the hidden agendas, meanings, and feelings that can get in the way of communication.

Unexpressed intentions and feelings can become a serious problem when the tension that accompanies them builds to the explosion point. Therefore, it is important to notice when such hidden elements may be coming into play, and to take them into consideration in responding to a message. In some cases—for example, when it is best for some reason not to provoke an open confrontation or airing of an issue—it may be necessary just to listen for the underlying meaning and use it to guide a decision. In other cases, it may be appropriate to find a comfortable way of bringing hidden elements to the surface and working with them more directly. The first step is to notice when another person is conveying some kind of concealed message. The second step is to decide what should be done about it and act accordingly.

Noticing Hidden Elements

The principal way of telling when there are hidden agendas, meanings, or feelings is to pay attention to discrepancies between nonverbal and verbal communication and to recognize the signs of such negative feelings as anger, resentment, jealousy, mistrust, and fear. Consider the following situations:

WORKSHEET 4

Communication Audit

Individuals or Groups from Whom to Get Information	Method of Providing Information (Indicate date, check once for "to do," twice for "done.")					
	Phone	Meeting	Memo	E-mail	Fax	Other

- *You feel in yourself a sense of distrust, distance, or negativity as you listen to or interact with another person.* Pay attention to these feelings. They could be a signal that the other person is saying one thing but really means, intends, or feels something else.

- *You notice signs of a discrepancy or disconnection between another person's message and his or her body language.* These signs may be gestures, tones, or movements that don't quite fit the words: a friendly smile accompanying a cold tone of voice; clenched hands; or a glance away from you, which suggests that the other person may not feel so warm toward you after all. Other signs include a hesitant or nervous manner and erratic eye contact accompanying any message, which are signs that the person may not be comfortable with what he or she is saying for whatever reason, and an aggressive tone and hard look, though the person tries to be reassuring and supportive, which suggest underlying hostility or blame.

Whatever the situation, and whatever your position in the organization, be attentive to these signs, and trust your feelings. Then base your best response on the circumstances.

Deciding What to Do About Hidden Elements

When you listen carefully to another person and pick up cues suggesting hidden messages that appear to contradict the overt message, the big question is what to do: how to get from the point of noticing to the point of responding, and how to respond. Should you check your perceptions out with the other person? Do you want to try to uncover the hidden feelings and meanings now? later? never? Once you have perceived an underlying content in a communication, you can consider taking one or more of the following actions:

- *Quietly pay attention to what you perceive, and "file" this perception for future reference.* This is a good strategy if you want to preserve the status quo for now. For example, perhaps you are in a low–status position, don't want to provoke a confrontation, like what you are doing despite your reservations about the other person, and have priorities more important than addressing this hidden message directly.

- *Discuss your concerns with someone you trust.* This is a good strategy if you want to know whether others have feelings similar to your own, or if you want advice about what to do. Before you share your perceptions, however, use caution. Make sure you can trust the other person—say, by hinting at your perceptions before you share them fully.

- *Discuss your perceptions with the other person directly, to bring these hidden elements out in the open.* This can be a good approach when you have been sensing these hidden issues for some time, feel that they are interfering with your own or others' work, and have some hope that the other person may be willing to listen to you and change. If you choose this strategy, be diplomatic and non-threatening, to make it easier for the other person to acknowledge and discuss the hidden elements. By opening the door in a comfortable, reassuring way, you give the other person an opportunity to address any underlying issues that may exist (and they usually do when you sense a disconnection or a discrepancy).

When you choose the strategy of direct discussion with the other person, you can gently describe your experience of the discrepancy. You can quietly explain that you are not convinced by what she is saying, or that you are confused by the difference between what she is saying and what you think she means, and that you hope to understand what she wants so that the two of you can work together more effectively. You can diplomatically say that you wonder whether there is some hostility, anger, resentment (or whatever else you detect) coming into play between you, and that you would like to try to resolve it. When you use this strategy, point out what the person has done or said to create the impression of a hidden element in the communication: "I thought you might be angry about something, because of the way you were so abrupt when I tried to speak to you. If so, I hope we can discuss whatever you may feel is a problem."

Chart 2 lists examples of statements that may have underlying meanings, as well as statements that can be used to uncover those meanings. You can use Worksheet 5 to list similar statements that apply to situations in your own experience.

CHART 2

Underlying Meanings: Statements and Strategies

What the Person Says	What You Think He or She Means	What You Might Say to Bring Out the Real Meanings or Feelings
"It's your project."	"I resent you for getting all the credit on this project, and you can't count on me for any further support."	"Would you like to be more involved? Maybe there are some ways we could work together to improve the project."
"It's up to you."	"I really would like to be involved. But I feel shut out and frustrated, since you have been ignoring my input."	"Do you have any suggestions for where we might go next? I really value your ideas."
"It's a done deal."	"I wish it weren't. But since it's done, I'm not going to put any more energy into this effort. You're on your own."	"It sounds like you may have some reservations. The project design may not be entirely final, if others have further input. Is there anything you'd like to suggest?
"I wasn't involved in the project."	"And am I ever glad I wasn't! It was a big mess, and I would never screw up like that. So if you'd like to work with someone who will do a better job in the future, consider me."	"But perhaps you know a little more about the project and how it was put together. Is there anything else you can tell me about it? I'd really like to hear your thoughts and opinions."

WORKSHEET 5

Underlying Meanings: Real-Life Statements and Strategies

What the Person Says	What You Think He or She Means	What You Might Say to Bring Out the Real Meanings or Feelings

HIDDEN OR FAULTY ASSUMPTIONS

We all form assumptions on the basis of our past experiences, and these assumptions usually serve as fairly good guides to future action. For example, you know your boss is very critical, so you take the extra time to polish a report, even though doing that means assigning a lower priority to something else. Or you know that an employee tends not to listen carefully, so you spend extra time repeating and clarifying your instructions.

These assumptions are often hidden in our communications with others. We don't take the time to notice them, spell them out, filter them out, or check them out. Remember, our assumptions are generally reliable; we trust them to guide our perceptions, and they free us to focus on what other people are saying or doing.

But what happens when assumptions are faulty? If they are sufficiently off base, or if you are unsure about whether they may be, it is a good idea to check them out. Then, if they are faulty, find out what actually is true. For example, maybe this time your boss is going to be less critical because meeting the deadline is more important than perfection. Maybe the employee who seems not to be listening has some distracting personal problems, and if you go into great detail in your instructions, you may unintentionally suggest that he is stupid, when what he really needs to improve his performance is some support from you.

Faulty assumptions are also a two-way street: another person may be operating on the basis of faulty assumptions about you or your behavior. Sometimes these assumptions will entail particular but unspoken expectations for what your behavior should be, as in the following example.

A Minor Misunderstanding
Leads to Prolonged Disharmony

Henry supervised a team of co-workers in a small company. All the team members got along very well in performing a variety of duties, which included promoting goodwill for the company. One such activity performed by Henry's team was organizing the company's annual holiday party, to which the most important community leaders were invited.

Kate, the team member who had assumed major responsibility for coordinating the previous parties, assumed that she would be in charge of this year's party as well. Therefore, she went about making all the usual arrangements—reserving a room, writing press releases, inviting community leaders, and so on—to make the party a success. What Kate didn't realize was that Henry had decided to get more involved this time, to the point of approving all the arrangements himself. At the planning meeting for the party, Kate had heard Henry express his wish for greater involvement, but she thought he simply wanted more frequent progress reports from her. Now Kate, with a large event in mind, spent hours making arrangements that she thought were final.

But Henry had other ideas—and Kate didn't realize it until Henry, with the help of several co-workers, had already made changes, about which he and the others informed her after the fact. This year's party, they said, would be a lower-key gathering, on the model of a social mixer.

Because Henry was her boss, Kate thought there was little she could say or do, and so she said nothing. But she was angry, disappointed, and demoralized. She also felt unappreciated and burned out. She cut back on her work for the party, and her feelings were carried over to her other work as well. As a result, her job performance suffered, and she seemed distant or irritable to her co-workers.

Only after Kate finally shared her feelings with one of her co-workers, who offered his appreciation and support, was she able to put the incident behind her. As for Henry, he really never did understand how more clarity about who was doing what could easily have prevented weeks of tension and lowered productivity.

Unconscious or faulty assumptions can work in much the same way that hidden agendas, meanings, and feelings do to undermine effective communication. Even though faulty assumptions operate in the realm of beliefs rather than emotion, they can still lead to negative feelings, as the preceding example has just shown. Here are some tips for avoiding faulty assumptions, noticing when they may be at work, and, as appropriate, taking action to correct them:

- *Clearly state your plans or intentions up front.* After you have done so (for example, at the planning meeting for some event), follow up with a phone call or a memo, and make sure that others acknowledge your plans and agree to these arrangements. And if you are planning a very large or important event or an event that is still far in the future, you may need additional follow-up.

- *Pay attention to the warning signs of wrong assumptions.* This way, you can step in early to correct errors if they seem serious or important enough to warrant action. Warning signs include people sharing information that you know is wrong or that doesn't sound correct; rumors or office scuttlebutt based on incorrect information; and unexpected or untimely actions or mistakes.

- *Check out uncertainties or information that sounds suspect.* Obviously, it is impossible to check out everything; in order to carry out our normal routines, we need to operate on some assumptions. At times, however, it is especially important to stop and ask yourself or others, "Is this correct?" For example, when you are using information to make an important decision, you want to be sure this information is accurate, so check your assumptions before you proceed.

- *Avoid jumping to wrong conclusions.* There are times for being spontaneous, but when a decision will bring big changes, or when a choice will have major consequences for the future, take extra time to make sure your assumptions are correct before you act. If there is any room for doubt or uncertainty, get more information.

- *If your assumptions about another person need to be checked out, take them to that person, and get direct feedback.* This checking can be easier to do when assumptions are task-oriented, as when you are assuming that someone is going to do something. It is more difficult to check when feelings are involved, as when you believe that someone with whom you are supposed to be working may not like or trust you and has been avoiding you. In either case, however, your goal is to have an open discussion to clear the air, using tact and diplomacy as necessary, so that the other person feels comfortable discussing any problems. This kind of openness leaves the way clear for any necessary apologies or new agreements, and it gets your working relationship back on course.

THE IMPORTANCE OF GOOD LISTENING

Good listening is the other half of good communication. If communication is like a waltz, in which the speaker leads and the listener follows, then a listener who doesn't follow is like a waltz partner who is doing the fox-trot, dancing out of time and stepping on her partner's feet.

Good listening, more than just listening to what someone is telling you, means responsively listening for unspoken messages by using the technique called *active listening* (see "Keys to Good Listening," p. 49). In active listening, you are truly present when another person communicates with you, and you react to demonstrate your presence. You listen with understanding and with interest in what the other person is telling you, and your behavior encourages the other person to communicate more fully, knowing that he or she has a receptive listener. If you are truly listening, you can also sense when the other person is giving communication-shutdown signals, perhaps because he or she doesn't want to go into further detail or is pressed by other time commitments. You can then respond appropriately, perhaps even waiting until another time if you need more information. The following case illustrates the importance of good listening skills.

Poor Listening Costs
Sam a Client

Sam, a freelance public relations consultant, was a fast-acting, big-picture person. He liked to figure out for himself the most efficient way of getting things done. This approach worked even with his more laid-back, analytical clients because he was so good at what he did. Then Sam worked for Larry.

To attract customers, Larry wanted to create his own newsletter, which would feature articles about his business activities. The year before, a newspaper had printed an interview with Larry; now Larry phoned Sam, told him he would send this interview to him that afternoon, and said he wanted Sam to revise it as an article written from Larry's point of view.

Sam, listening to Larry, knew at once just how he would approach this task: change the point of view, reorganize, tighten the style. When Larry mentioned that in a few days he would also send Sam copies of some other pieces he had written, Sam jumped to the conclusion that these were meant for future articles. He didn't hear Larry ask him to hold off on writing the first article until he had received the other pieces, which were to be used in adapting the interview to Larry's style.

Sam got the interview in the next day's mail and quickly reworked it, taking pride in his speed. But when Larry read the new article, he was very upset. He felt that it lacked his voice—and, more, that Sam hadn't taken him seriously, since he hadn't waited to write it.

Sam had to rewrite the article without charging Larry. He also had to deal with Larry's anger and disappointment over not having been listened to. Larry found someone else to do his future public relations work for him—not because Sam couldn't do the job, but because Sam's impatience had stood in the way of his fully hearing what Larry really wanted.

Keys to
Good Listening

The receptive, nonjudgmental technique known as *active listening* has the advantage of giving the other person time and space to release feelings. He or she will then feel better, and you will have a better idea of just what he or she is feeling. Later on, with this knowledge, you will be better able to address the other person's concerns—say, by changing your own behavior as an employee, changing your expectations and demands as an employer, or altering the way you relate to this person as a co-worker, if these changes seem warranted by the circumstances. As you listen and gain insight, keep the following points in mind:

- *Answer the other person's questions as openly and honestly as possible.* The key here is to provide information that may help the person feel better about the situation or about his or her role

in it. Even if this information confirms his or her fears or suspicions, the fact that you are sharing it can help the person
understand what is causing the situation and make choices
about what to do.

- *Act calm and stay calm, even when the other person raises uncomfortable questions or uses an angry, hostile, or suspicious tone.* That way,
  you won't let yourself be dragged into an emotional confrontation with someone who is already emotional, and you defuse
  his or her emotional energy instead of adding it to your own.

- *Listen patiently, and be reassuring.* This gives the other person
  space to release feelings without pressure. That way, the person
  is encouraged to trust you, and you get more of the information you need to solve the problem—not to mention more of
  the other person's cooperation in solving it.

- *Be present and attentive—or explain if you aren't able to pay full
  attention.* If you can't be "all there," the other person will generally sense your inattention and perceive you as uninterested
  or insincere. He or she may then feel insulted, angry, or resentful. If for some reason you're distracted from listening, explain
  why: "I'm expecting someone in a few minutes, so I'm sorry if
  I may have to look away from time to time as we talk." If necessary, ask if your conversation with the other person can take
  place at another time, when you can give your full attention.

- *Listen for feelings as well as content.* That way, you can pick up any
  underlying or hidden messages and decide how best to approach them. In everyday situations that are free of conflict,
  what people say is usually congruent with what they mean or
  feel. An incongruity may be revealed by a person's tone, body
  language, use or avoidance of eye contact, and other signals.

- *Reflect back what you are hearing.* Doing this shows that you are
  paying attention and trying to understand what the other
  person is saying. It also gives you a chance to correct any misunderstandings before they get worse, and it helps keep the
  conversation on track. Don't overdo this reflection process,
  however. The point is not to be an echo or slow the conversation down. Rather, from time to time, summarize or para-

phrase what you have just heard the other person say: "I understand that you're interested in . . ." or "I understand that you believe . . . ." You can also use this technique if you sense underlying, unspoken messages suggesting that the other person has negative feelings. (Here, though, consider whether it might be better to wait until later to talk about them.) If you choose to confront these feelings directly, be tactful: "I sense that you might be feeling . . ." or "It sounds as if you might feel that . . . ." As appropriate, emphasize that you want to promote understanding and a good relationship between the two of you. Then, as you describe your perceptions, notice whether the other person seems receptive. If he or she seems uncomfortable, back off. And, at least as important, invite the other person to let you know if your perceptions are correct.

- *Use nonverbal listening responses to show your interest and empathy.* These responses help to show that you want the other person to keep talking. As appropriate, you can smile, lean toward the speaker, nod, and make eye contact. You can also use essentially nonverbal sounds—"Uh-humm," "Yeah, right"— to show that you are listening and want the other person to go on.

- *Ask questions to clarify what you are unsure about or don't understand.* If the other person says things that aren't clear or that don't sound correct to you, diplomatically ask for more explanation, since you don't understand. Otherwise, the other person may think you understand when you don't, and a conflict could erupt later.

- *Ask open-ended questions to encourage further discussion and explanation.* An open-ended question is one that cannot be answered with "yes" or "no" or with a single factual statement. Such questions let the other person decide what and how much to say: "Can you tell me a little more about this?" "How did you feel/react when that happened?"

PART 2

WORKING WITH REASON

Reason, the second element of the ERI model, plays an important role in helping you deal with difficult situations. It allows you to do two fundamental things: recognize the factors that may be contributing to a particular situation, and use an appropriate strategy for approaching and resolving the situation.

Each situation is different, of course, and is influenced by a number of variables. These include political factors (such as differences in individuals' power), factors arising from an organization's culture, or factors connected with the interests, wants, and needs of the people involved in the situation (Chapter 4). Another set of factors involves the particular personalities of the people involved in the situation, some of whom may be difficult to work with (Chapter 5). An important variable is the conflict style that will be most appropriate to a particular situation (Chapter 6). Finally, the outcome of any situation will be heavily influenced by the negotiation skills and strategies brought to bear on it (Chapter 7).

CHAPTER 4

Analyzing Organizational and Individual Factors

$\mathbf{A}$s you use the ERI model to resolve conflicts and work with other kinds of difficult situations, you will need to use your reason in cultivating an awareness of three kinds of organizational factors: organizational culture, organizational politics, and the individual stakes, or interests, that people have in various kinds of outcomes. *Organizational culture* has to do with such factors as a company's traditional way of doing things, its rules and regulations, its official policies, and its unwritten rules for deviating from any of these norms. *Organizational politics* involve the power relationships between individuals or between groups in the organization who forms various kinds of alignments (who may be that individual or group's allies or enemies, or who may be neutral or simply uninvolved). No matter what your position in the organization may be, there is no escape from the organization's culture or politics, which form the context for any difficult situation that arises at work. Therefore, this context always forms the *cultural* or *political dimension* of the difficulty, no matter how different this situation may be from others. In addition, all members in an organization have *individual* interests that are shaped by the organization's cultural and political environments; for example, your interests will be affected by your position in the organization or your relationships with others. But you will have personal interests as well, shaped by your own desires and needs; for that reason, we will refer to them here as individual *interests, wants, and needs,* or *IWNs.*

ASSESSING THE ORGANIZATION'S CULTURAL AND POLITICAL ENVIRONMENTS

If you have an understanding of your organization's cultural and political environments, you can avoid falling into some kinds of difficult situations—or, if you have fallen in, you may be able to get out more easily. Often, however, we don't pay attention to cultural and political factors. We take them for granted, or we don't notice that they have changed until a problem develops, as in the following case.

A Sales Rep Considers a Lawsuit

Frances was a sales representative for a trade council that had the goal of bringing businesses of all types together in productive trade arrangements—local, national, and global. Her job was to make contact with businesses that were potential clients and persuade them to sign up as members of the council.

With five years' experience, Frances was the most senior member of the sales team. Even her boss, Anthony, had been with the council for only three years. More and more, however, Frances was finding that the newer sales reps were more successful than she was, and she was upset: she had once been the most productive member of the sales group.

As Frances understood the situation, some of the more aggressive new reps were stealing her leads. For example, when prospective members phoned the council and left messages for her, these reps were quick to intercept the messages and return these prospects' calls. The reps also picked up the business cards that prospects left at the council's social mixers and educational meetings—cards that Frances thought should have gone to her. Worse, Frances felt that Anthony not only was unsupportive of her but was seeking to undermine her by throwing his support behind these newer reps. His motive, she thought, was racism: Frances was African American, whereas most of the newer sales reps, all hired by Anthony, were white or Asian American.

Frances spoke with a civil rights attorney about the possibility of filing suit. The attorney encouraged her to gather evidence, and

Frances began to document occasions when other sales reps stole her leads. She also took note of Anthony's praise for the other reps, documenting it as a sign of his racist attitudes.

Over the next few weeks, Frances—seeing herself in a "me versus them" situation and fighting to keep her job—became less and less of a team player and grew more combative in her relationships at work. She was increasingly pushy in her contacts with prospective clients, too, and her behavior alienated some of them. Moreover, as she concentrated on documenting offenses and talking with her lawyer, she became less productive. In fact, preoccupied as she was with preparing her lawsuit, she had less time available for seeing prospective clients, and so the other sales reps began to take even more of her leads—with Anthony's full encouragement.

Frances was now a few days away from having her lawyer file suit, and from leaving what had been a good and satisfying job up to the point when she had concluded that Anthony was a racist. But was he a racist? And even if he was, should she leave? Fortunately, Frances had a chance to discuss the issue with some friends and associates, who were able to see the situation in a more objective way. As a result, she recognized how she had enjoyed her work before falling into this conflict with her boss and the other sales reps, so she decided to call off her lawyer and try to work things out.

Taking this time out to reflect on her situation led her to see that racism was an unlikely explanation for what was occurring: the trade council was, after all, a multiracial organization that dealt with business leaders from a variety of ethnic and racial backgrounds, in the United States and abroad. Frances had achieved her earlier success by being very aggressive and assertive. Was it possible, she now wondered, that she had made Anthony uncomfortable with her high-energy style? Could it be that the other sales reps, seeing that she had not picked up Anthony's cue to be more subdued in contacting prospective clients, were taking advantage of her failure to adapt? If so, then her assessment of her boss's motives was wrong.

Frances decided that the solution was not to file a lawsuit. Instead, she chose to work on mending fences with Anthony and her co-workers, and to rework her style to fit what had become the more restrained culture of the organization. Over time, this conflict was resolved, and as Frances became more of a team player, she got more leads—and soon found herself once again at the top of the sales team.

Attention to cultural and political dynamics in the organization can alert you to signs that conditions are changing in ways that may lead to conflict. Then, if a problem does occur, your awareness of the cultural and political dimensions can help you assess any underlying factors that may be contributing to it—for example, conflicting organizational rules and priorities, or disputes over work roles and responsibilities. Your awareness of these dimensions can also help you know when to make changes in the organization if you are in a position to name them, and when to make changes in your own approach to adapt to organizational realities. This awareness will also help you decide when to leave the organization because there is no longer a good fit between its style or goals and your own. If a difficult situation has developed in your organization, you can use Worksheet 6 to think it through from the perspective of organizational culture and politics. You can use Worksheet 7 to review your perceptions of your organization and consider various possibilities for explaining your observations.

ASSESSING AND WORKING WITH INTERESTS, WANTS, AND NEEDS

A good salesperson, making a pitch to a prospective customer and trying to find the potential buyer's "hot buttons," is very much aware of IWNs. Likewise, effective politicians adopt and modify their positions on the basis of what they think voters want or need. You, too, whenever your goal is to persuade another person to think, feel, or act in a certain way, must consider that person's IWNs as you pursue your goal. That way, you are also more likely to satisfy your own IWNs.

In a simple one-to-one interaction, you need only consider the IWNs of two parties: the other person and yourself. What appears to be a simple one-to-one relationship may actually be more complex, however, in that one or both of you may also have to satisfy the IWNs of multiple other parties, and these IWNs will vary in their importance to you and the other party. Moreover, you both may be expressing certain IWNs, but there may be others that are deeper and left unexpressed, alongside unexpressed fears and worries. A further consideration is the degree to which each party is responsible for taking action to address these IWNs. Particularly in a larger organization,

WORKSHEET 6

Analyzing Cultural and Political Factors

Cultural and Political Factors	Circumstances in My Situation	Importance of Different Factors
What is usually done		
Usual rules and regulations that apply		
My own level of power, compared to the level of power of other(s) involved		
My length of time with the organization, compared to the length of time of others		
My allies, supporters, and opponents, compared to the allies, supporters, and opponents of others		
Other factors in the environment that might be having an effect		

WORKSHEET 7

Analyzing Perceptions and Possibilities

Problems in My Relationships with Others in the Organization	What I Believe Are the Motives of Those Involved	Other Possible Motives

this can be a very fuzzy issue and may sometimes contribute to the creation of a difficult situation: the classic passing of the buck. To solve the problem, you have to find someone who will take action—you usually do this by appealing to that person's own IWNs—and that action can then break the cycle and trigger other actions. The key is to intervene at that point in the cycle where intervention will start a series of actions. Your understanding of the interests, wants, and needs of everyone involved can guide you in finding when and where to intervene.

Responding to Interests, Wants, and Needs

When you take the interests, wants, and needs of others into account, you also help yourself achieve your own goals, as the following case illustrates.

Political Sensitivity
Makes the Difference

Arne had been working as a clerk in a large, bureaucratic city agency responsible for enforcing compliance with environmental regulations. He hoped to advance to a position in the agency's research department, but he didn't have the formal training or credentials for a promotion to that level. Nevertheless, he thought that he might be able to bypass the usual procedures for testing and promotion if he were to do a research project on his own time, after hours and on weekends, in an area where the city had a clear interest. This project, once completed, would show that he was capable of doing research, and he thought the recognition the project would bring might be enough to get him the desired promotion.

Arne chose environmental hazards in the city for his research topic. He thought that information in this area would be of wide general interest and could help city officials and community members make improvements where such hazards existed. He even persuaded the chief of the agency's records department to give him access to some semipublic files, and he promised to keep sensitive information confidential. To ensure the continued support of the records chief, Arne agreed to show him drafts of the report as it developed, and he honored this agreement over the course of the twelve months that he worked on his project.

When Arne finished his report, he made copies for his own supervisor and for the head of the agency. Coincidentally, just as Arne submitted this report, the city's major newspaper began a series on environmental hazards. Arne thought that now there would be more public interest in this topic than ever. He envisioned himself doing public presentations on the agency's behalf about environmental hazards, and he proposed that the agency let him organize a citywide event where he could make the first such presentation.

But a number of people in the agency had different ideas, which were based on their different interests:

• The head of the agency was reluctant to let Arne make presentations on environmental hazards, already a sensitive topic. Arne tried to give assurances that his goal was simply to point out ways in which the city might improve its efforts and involve citizens, but the agency head was not sure that Arne had the skills to do a good job, and he feared that the research results, if negative, about the agency's activities might make the agency look bad. He also thought that if the report were made public, it should be presented as an agency report; or, alternatively, that if Arne were given credit, the credit should be shared with the records chief, since Arne's research had been done with the chief's cooperation and the city's own records.

• The head of the agency's public relations department thought that Arne's research project would make for a good human-interest story about an idealistic, ambitious clerk rising against the odds and outside the system. At the same time, the PR head wanted to avoid appearing indifferent to the concerns of the agency head.

• Arne's supervisor wanted her department to get some credit for what Arne had done, so that her department would look good and Arne's project would not appear to be his way of going over her head in his quest for a promotion.

Thus Arne's solid, comprehensive report did more than raise awareness of environmental hazards. It also raised multiple concerns of a delicate nature among various interested parties within the agency.

Arne felt that he had to be sensitive to the personal politics of the situation, not only to advance within the agency but also to protect his current position. He knew that he could jeopardize both if he acted too forcefully to promote his own interests or failed to consider others' concerns—those that they had already expressed openly, and those that might be unspoken but were just as real.

In the end, a series of meetings among the parties involved led to the decision that Arne and the research chief would give a joint "pilot" presentation of Arne's findings to a small group of city employees, without press coverage. This presentation was a great success. The agency head was reassured that Arne would do a good job and that his report presented a favorable view of the agency's performance. The PR head saw that Arne's findings could be used to show how the agency was taking action to fight environmental hazards. Arne's supervisor felt validated when she was praised for her management of an employee who went the extra mile.

The situation was still not completely resolved, however: the question was raised again of whether Arne should be given sole credit for the research project and the report. After much discussion, it was decided that credit should be shared with the research chief.

At first Arne felt frustrated by this decision. The work was, after all, his own; if he had been a journalist or an academic researcher, there would have been no question whatsoever of his taking sole credit. He was also legally entitled at any time to release his findings to the media or publish them under his own name. Nevertheless, Arne agreed to this arrangement, wanting to be sure that everyone felt comfortable, and he renounced the thought of making future presentations on his own without the agency's approval. He also told the research chief that he would refrain from making any contact with the press; that, Arne said, would be up to the research chief, as would any future presentations.

Difficult though this gesture was for Arne, it was also exactly the right thing for him to do. The research chief, gratified at first by the shared credit, soon began to realize how much extra work he would be taking on by doing a series of presentations with Arne. He also realized that he was not entirely comfortable with the idea of taking credit for Arne's work.

In the end, the research chief, forgoing shared credit, decided that he would be pleased just to have his department's assistance acknowledged. Arne received approval to present the report on his own and, after making several presentations, was able to step into the research position that he had imagined and then created for himself.

You may need, as Arne did, to change or adapt your objectives, or to take more time in achieving them. If you build with the concerns of others in mind, however, what you build is likely to last longer and be more satisfying to you and everyone else, and this is true whether you seek to fulfill a career goal, settle a dispute, or manage a negotiation.

To assess the various IWNs of the people in your organizational environment, ask yourself questions like the ones that follow, filling in the blanks with people's names:

- What does _____ state as his/her main goals, desires, or needs at this time?

- What other goals, desires, or needs might _____ have?

- Might _____ have any unexpressed or hidden goals, desires, or needs?

- How could what I want benefit _____?

- Are there other ways in which my goals might benefit _____?

- How can I demonstrate these benefits to _____?

- How can I relate these added benefits to _____'s goals, desires, or needs?

As you demonstrate that your goals are compatible with the goals of others, or as you adapt your goals to benefit them, taking into account their IWNs, you increase the likelihood that you will get what you want. Worksheets 8 and 9 can help you begin this kind of assessment.

Noticing Alignments and Oppositions

When you have a sense of others' IWNs, you can assess the extent to which they are aligned with, opposed to, or independent of your own. You can then think about ways of securing support from people whose IWNs are aligned with or independent of yours, and of winning over people whose IWNs are opposed to yours. You can also devise strategies for adapting your goals to incorporate the IWNs of other people, so that others will support you. You are able, in effect, to approach situations in much the same way that politicians do when they seek support and create coalitions to achieve their goals.

WORKSHEET 8

Assessing Interests, Wants, and Needs

The difficult situation I am trying to resolve:

_____

_____

Interests, Wants, and Needs

Individuals in the Situation	Primary Stated Interests, Wants, and Needs	Other Stated Interests, Wants, and Needs	Possible Hidden Interests, Wants, and Needs
Myself			
Most important person or group to satisfy			
Next most important person or group			
Next most Important person or group			
Others involved in the situation			

What can I do to meet the interests, wants, and needs of these individuals?

_____

WORKSHEET 9

Assessing the Benefits of My Interests, Wants, and Needs

The difficult situation I am trying to resolve:

_____

_____

Benefits Offered by What I Want

Others in the Situation	Types of Benefits	Relationship of Benefits to Goals	How I Can Demonstrate Benefits
Most important person or group to satisfy			
Next most important person or group to satisfy			
Next most important person or group			
Additional people involved in the situation			

While you may hope for balance and harmony in resolving a conflict and restoring good working relationships with others, any conflict is much like a battle or a political challenge. The parties on both sides are trying to achieve certain goals and objectives, with different ideas about what the outcome should be, how it should be achieved, or both. The eventual resolution, whatever it is, will inevitably represent more of a win or a loss for you, as well as for the other parties, or it could be turned into a win-win situation for all parties. The value of the outcome to you and others depends on how well it fits in with your differing goals and objectives.

So it is in war and politics. This is why before they go into battle, military commanders determine whether the battle is important enough to fight and whether they have the resources and the will to win. You should do the same: weigh your strength, and choose your battles. A key variable will be whether the organization's cultural and political climates, as they exist now, favor your chances of prevailing. Where do you stand, in comparison with others, in terms of organizational power? Do others support your position? If so, how powerful are your supporters? How powerful are your opponents? If it seems likely that you will prevail or have a positive effect in shaping the outcome, it's worth engaging in battle; if not, retreat and, if the battle remains important, wait for a more opportune time.

In short, then, before you choose to do battle in a particular situation, be aware of the organizational environment around you and take it into account as you assess your odds of winning. If you fail to take this step, you will find it more difficult to resolve the situation to your own satisfaction because you will be unprepared for the factors working against your interests and therefore less likely to win. Also, if your assessment indicates that you are likely to lose the battle, you can back down or walk away and avoid losing face as well.

The following two examples illustrate why it is crucial to be aware of the organizational and power dynamics that affect your position in the organization and act accordingly.

Assessing the Environment
Leads to a Wise Decision

When Dan applied for a job as a sales rep for a company with a new high-tech product, Ted, the sales manager, waxed enthusiastic over Dan's previous experience as a rep for another company, spoke glowingly about the high commissions and draw Dan was to receive, and invited him to start right away. He promised he would have a contract for Dan very soon, but in the meantime, Ted asked Dan to compile a list of the leads he planned to contact.

At first, Dan plunged into the project enthusiastically, using the company's computer to search the Internet for leads, but after a few days he began asking Ted about the contract that would formalize their understanding about his percentages. Also, he began to worry about the work he was doing without a contract, although Ted assured him the contract was "on the way through channels" and asked him to keep going. Dan would certainly have the contract before he started selling. But Dan was concerned, and as a result, he began talking to the other newly hired sales reps and to a few employees from other departments he met in the company cafeteria.

Gradually, as he spoke with others, Dan began to realize that the company was in a shaky position, and he learned that the sales manager, Ted, was newly hired, too. In fact, as one employee told him, the company was still undecided about whether it wanted to fully commit itself to this new product line, and so it was testing the waters.

Dan discovered that he was being asked to work in a highly uncertain, speculative situation, based on a promise for a job that might or might not materialize. In the meantime, the company was taking advantage of him, getting Dan to gather some of the preliminary information it needed to make its decision, rather than hiring someone to do this and then bringing in a sales team if it decided to go forward. Dan also feared that if he continued to work without payment or a contract, the sales manager could take advantage of him further by offering him a lower commission or draw than he had promised verbally. He might think Dan would be willing to take less, since he had already invested too much time in the project to walk away from even a lesser offer. In addition, Dan felt that if the sales manager had breached his trust now, the work environment might prove to be one in which trust was a problem generally.

On the basis of all these factors, Dan decided to turn down the position. He felt it was better to write off the ten hours or so he had already spent than to take any further chances with a company and a manager he couldn't trust. Subsequently, Dan learned through his network of friends in sales that the company never did do well with the product line. It got an unpaid sales force to do its market research and then never gave the line its full marketing and promotional support. So Dan would never have been able to make a good commission had he stayed. Thus he did well to back out of the project.

A Sales Rep Misreads an Opportunity

By contrast, Susan stuck it out as sales rep at her company because she wanted to believe that conditions would get better. Although business was not going well at the moment, her sales manager kept talking about plans for a reorganization, which would improve the company's sales territories, and hinted that new, more profitable lines of products were coming. If only Susan would stay with the company for the next few months, she would be in line for a big promotion and increased commission.

So Susan stayed with the company, ignoring the warning signs of the serious problems her sales manager tried to cover up, including major uncertainties in the market. The longer she stayed and the more time she invested, the more reluctant she was to leave. When other sales reps started leaving the company, she interpreted it to mean that she would be in a position to get a better territory when the reorganization occurred and the new product lines were introduced.

But Susan was putting on blinders and failing to correctly assess the social and business environment of the situation. The company was in serious trouble, though her sales manager sought to conceal this, and when the reorganization finally occurred, there were actually *fewer* opportunities for the sales force. Sales had become more technology oriented, with the customers making more of their choices by computer rather than buying through the sales reps. Instead of focusing on improving her position in sales, Susan would have done better to recognize how the company was changing and invest her energies in learning new skills and perhaps transferring into another department where she could advance more successfully.

Once you decide to go ahead and do battle in a difficult situation, you will need a strategy, just as a general needs a strategy in organizing a military battle. For ideas that can help you understand the cultural and political factors in your organization, spot and prevent potential conflicts, or productively resolve them when they can't be prevented, see "Choosing a Strategy" on page 70.

Choosing a Strategy

As you experience and respond to difficult situations in your workplace, you may find some or all of the following suggestions helpful in gaining insight into the cultural or political factors affecting them.

- *Make an organizational chart.* Use or adapt the diagram shown in Figure 3 (p. 70) to make a chart of your organization and the various people with whom you work. Use special symbols to designate different groups of people (for example, use triangles to indicate men and circles to indicate women) and set up your chart in the form of a pyramid, with the more powerful people at or near the top and the less powerful people at or near the base. If yours is a very hierarchical organization, make the pyramid a steep one; if it is a fairly egalitarian organization, make the pyramid less steep. You can also use an unbroken line to indicate an ongoing direct relationship between two people, a broken line to indicate an occasional direct relationship, and an arrow to indicate the flow of power. Use a unidirectional arrow to show a hierarchical relationship and a two-way arrow to show a more egalitarian relationship. Use a distinctive shape to indicate your own position, and include only those other positions that are relevant to your own in the conflict situation you are mapping. As you examine the chart, note any special conditions that may be affecting the organizational climate. For example, if close friendships or power alliances connect two or more individuals, link those individuals with the symbol =. If someone in a higher position doesn't actually exercise the power that goes with that position, note this circumstance with a small *p* to indicate low power.

- *Establish a relationship with a higher-up.* Find a mentor you can trust, and share your perceptions of the organization, asking for feedback on your accuracy. Your mentor will probably have a bigger picture of the organization's cultural and political environments, and if you share your concerns in a positive way, with a view to making your own role in the organization more productive, your mentor may be able to give you helpful advice. It's important, however, not to gripe or complain to your mentor: his or her first loyalty will be to the organization as a whole, and if you come across as a whiner or complainer, you risk having your mentor see you as a problem for the company. An occasional observation about problems may be fine, but don't overdo it. Rather, focus on what you can do to improve any problems and how your mentor can help you do this.

- *Maintain an awareness of personality factors.* Various alignments and oppositions already exist among the people in your organization. Take note of these alignments and oppositions so that you can make use of them if you need to. You can simply list them, or add them to your organizational chart. By being aware, you can take advantage of existing alignments and more easily avoid potential conflicts when you make assignments or assemble teams. Information about alignments and oppositions can also be helpful in a dispute, when you want to find out what's wrong or attempt to gain support for your point of view. For example, after you have talked with one person in a group of allies, you can, with that person's permission, use information from this conversation in talking with someone else in that group, who in turn will feel more comfortable talking with you and supporting you. Take care, however, to conduct these conversations in such a way that you don't appear unduly aligned with a particular faction; for example, have individual conversations with members of a team or alliance rather than meeting with all of them as a group.

- *Notice discrepancies between organizational rules and realities.* Ask yourself if there are serious disconnections between official organizational policies, procedures, values, norms, objectives, purposes, or missions, on the one hand, and what people are actually doing, on the other. Whether such discrepancies are serious or not, they exist to some degree in every organization, and flexibility is usually fine, within limits. But if the gap between what is officially done and what is actually done seems to be large or growing wider, pay attention: this gap is analogous to a fault line, and the tension could be released in an organizational earthquake. See if there is some way to intervene before the discrepancy produces overt conflict. For example, if you are the head of a department where a gap of this kind is widening, call a meeting. Point out the split, and set new guidelines that will be followed more closely.

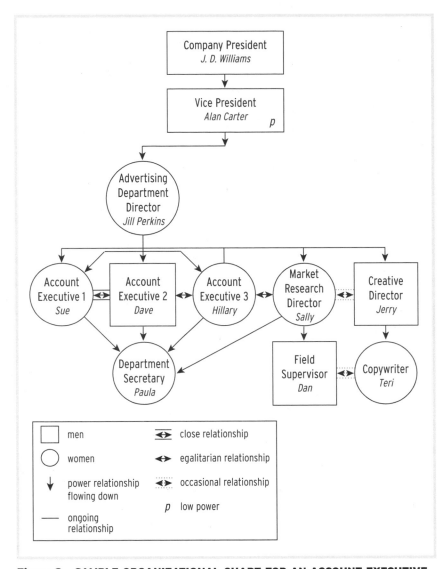

Figure 3   SAMPLE ORGANIZATIONAL CHART FOR AN ACCOUNT EXECUTIVE

CHAPTER 5

Working with
Difficult People

In the previous chapter, we saw how reason can be used to analyze the interests, wants, and needs of the people in an organization. As you seek to resolve conflicts and other kinds of difficult situations, you can use this chapter for help in working with another factor: difficult people in all their variety.

You may be somewhat more likely to find the power-driven types at or near the top of the organizational hierarchy. As people get promoted, however, they carry their styles with them, and so you can find any type anywhere in the organization. It is also important to remember that people may combine different types of difficult behavior, or they may take on different characteristics at different times and in different circumstances. For instance, someone may try hard to charm higher-ups; with co-workers and underlings, however, the same person may be more aggressive and irascible.

The descriptions that follow alternate between the use of "he" and "she" as a generic pronoun, but any of the characteristics may be displayed by people of either gender. And if you find that the description of a particular type of difficult person fits you and your behavior, you may want to think about that. Is your behavior creating any problems for you in your relationships at work? Is it interfering with your productivity? If so, you can consider how you might change—particularly if you notice that others are using the "difficult people" strategies described here in their dealings with you!

EMOTIONAL DRAINS

Some people are difficult primarily because they respond to situations in various kinds of emotional ways. They may behave in these ways because they find themselves toward the lower end of the power spectrum and thus feel angry, resentful, or hurt because they don't get enough recognition, support, or cooperation, or they may feel other kinds of deprivation because of their low status. Of course, there are also people at higher levels who become emotional when they are upset; the classic example is the boss who erupts like a volcano when angered by what an employee has done wrong. But being too emotional can be a barrier to rising in the organization. As a result, many of the types described in this section are stuck near the bottom—unless they are extremely creative or happen to own the company, in which case they may be found at or near the top.

The Exploder

This kind of person doesn't just get angry. She gets furious and explodes, like a child having a tantrum. The Exploder commonly reacts in this manner because she feels very frustrated or fearful, and this is her way of gaining control—and, she hopes, getting her own way.

Let's say that the Exploder has put a great deal of energy and effort into a report, only to be told at the end that the company is going in another direction, and so her report won't be needed. Most people in this situation would feel frustrated and upset, but they would hold their feelings back or share their upset privately with a friend at work or at home. The Exploder literally can't contain her anger. When she hears the bad news, she erupts in front of the person responsible for the decision that has provoked her anger, or she blows up at others who are nearby.

To some extent, the appropriate response to an Exploder depends on your relationship with her. If you are her employer, you may choose to terminate her for being disruptive, unless there are other reasons for retaining her (if, for example, she is a very good employee most of the time). If the Exploder is your boss, you may be willing to listen and take it, knowing that most of the time your boss is rational and that conditions are otherwise good. As a co-worker of the Exploder, you may seek to work with her less often. In general, however, the way to deal with being on the receiving end of an Exploder's tirade is to avoid escalation.

One strategy is to walk away until the Exploder calms down—unless she is your boss, in which case you may listen quietly (or act as if you are listening) but tune out what the Exploder is saying until her fury is spent. That way, you won't get upset and emotional yourself.

Another strategy is to listen stoically and let the Exploder finish venting her feelings. Then, when she is calm again, act as if she is an ordinary, reasonable person—as if the tantrum never happened.

You can also indicate to the Exploder, calmly and politely, that you are open to talking about the problem, if she wants to do that. This strategy can be effective because the Exploder is often embarrassed and apologetic after a blowup.

If the Exploder offers an apology, accept it, to help her feel better. Otherwise, though, it's usually best to shift the focus away from the incident, since the Exploder is likely to want to forget it ever happened. Once back in control, she would rather be seen as a responsible, rational adult, so help her feel that way, as best you can, and move on, putting the incident in the past.

The Complainer

There are two types of complainers: the Realistic Complainer, and the Paranoid Complainer who imagines slights or exaggerates problems. In either case, the Complainer is frequently griping about something and blaming others—specific people, the organization, or the system in general. Complaining can sometimes be productive, of course: when it points to an identifiable problem that can realistically be solved, and when it leads to appropriate action. Typically, however, the Complainer magnifies problems, finds problems where none exist, or contributes to the creation of problems—and then complains.

The Complainer may be someone who is afraid of changes in the organization or in his style of doing business, and so he complains because he feels that something is likely to go wrong, or he blames someone else for not carrying out the changes properly. Or the Complainer may repeatedly whine about the way a boss or a co-worker is doing her job, finding fault in many things that she does. Whatever the situation, the Complainer can usually find something to complain about, since he looks at the world through pessimistic glasses.

The Complainer will often unload to you about the situation in general because you seem willing to listen. Sometimes, however, the Complainer will attack you for something you actually did or for which he blames you.

Either way, you usually don't have to take these complaints too seriously, since the Complainer is probably griping to let off steam rather than expecting any constructive action to result from his complaints.

The key to dealing with the Complainer is to listen, whether or not you think his complaints are unfounded. That way, you give the Complainer a chance to be heard, as well as a feeling of power and a place to discharge his frustration. A good technique is to use reflective listening: in your own words, you repeat what you heard the Complainer say, or you give a capsule description of what you heard him say. Thus you acknowledge or validate what the Complainer is saying: you show that you have heard and understood, and you show your respect by listening, whether or not you agree with the complaints. After the Complainer has poured out his basic complaint, seek closure. Try to shift to a problem-solving approach. Ask him what he might want to do to in order to solve the problem. Are there others who might help in solving it? And, if the Complainer is blaming you for something, ask what you can do together to find some resolution. In short, acknowledge his complaint, and then move on. A benefit of using this approach, in which you shift quickly from a focus on problems to a focus on solutions, is that the Complainer will either cheer up and stop complaining (at least for now) or find somebody else to gripe to. Either way, you move on.

The Sulker

The Sulker is another extreme emotional type. The Sulker acts distant, but she won't tell you why. You feel that she is suddenly avoiding you. You notice a tension or reserve in her expression, and you feel that there is some barrier to communication, but she offers no explanation, and she denies that there's a problem if you ask. Or you find her door closed, or she is "missing in action" when there are tasks that need to be done.

The Sulker is behaving in this manner because it's her way of coping with a situation that is making her angry or upset. Her way is to quietly heal on her own or avoid the problem. The Sulker is like a turtle retreating into its shell until the threat of danger passes.

The farther down the organizational ladder the Sulker is, the riskier this response becomes: when someone with little status or power uses this approach, others may find it easy to ignore her or cut her out of the loop. Then she can't perform well, and it becomes easy to terminate her for not doing a good job. The Sulker may also find that she can't continue sulking when she is confronted by an angry boss; if she does, she is likely to be fired. By contrast, a Sulker who has more power can use this approach to withdraw from a problem until she has developed a strategy or the problem has resolved itself. Because the more powerful Sulker's contribution is valued more, others are more willing to ride out her period of gloom.

In any case, if a Sulker is giving you the silent treatment, one strategy is to be patient and wait, if you can, for the Sulker to come out of her shell. If you hope to work through the problem now, however, don't confront the Sulker by directly asking what's wrong or nagging and begging her to tell you about the problem. This approach is likely to make the Sulker even more defensive and send her even farther into her shell. Try instead to create a sympathetic, nurturing environment that encourages the Sulker to talk and gradually open up. Ask open-ended questions: "What's your thinking on that?" Or, in a low-key, nonjudgmental way, allude to what you think the problem is: "You've seemed a little hard to reach over the last few days. I was concerned that you might have some reservations about the project we discussed last week. And if anything's bothering you, maybe I can do something to help."

This gentle, nurturing response can work because the Sulker is often afraid to own up to negative feelings or to do anything wrong. Therefore, don't rush the Sulker's responses, and don't seek to fill the silence while you're waiting for an answer. Rather, if and when the Sulker begins to open up, even a little, let her know that you appreciate her discussing the issue or trying to deal with the problem, whether or not you agree with what she says about it. The idea is to bring the Sulker out and get her talking and, one hopes, over her sulking.

When the Sulker begins to respond, back off as soon as you feel any new resistance. Be patient. It may take several conversations to get to the bottom of the problem and solve it. But when the Sulker has other good qualities, the solution can be worth waiting for. Reconsider, though, if the Sulker is sulking too much; continuing to work with her may not be worth the effort.

The Sensitive Soul

This person goes by a number of names. Basically, however, the Sensitive Soul is highly reactive to any hint of disagreement or criticism, or to any suggestion that he may be wrong or may have made a mistake. He reacts in this way because he has a deep-seated sense of inferiority. Should the Sensitive Soul feel disparaged or disrespected, he is likely to feel hurt and angry and may turn into an Exploder or a Sulker.

Like the other types discussed in this section, the Sensitive Soul is typically found at the lower levels of the organization: after all, being a successful player in organizational politics takes a fairly thick skin. Nevertheless, the Sensitive Soul may be able to flourish and advance in an organization that deals with an arts- or entertainment-oriented field, where creativity and connections may help to offset the disadvantages of hypersensitivity.

One good approach to the Sensitive Soul is to try supporting and humoring him. That way, you help him feel better about himself, and you show that he is respected and valued, and so he feels less need for self-protection. This approach is particularly useful in a crisis, whether the Sensitive Soul is upset by you or by someone else. With the crisis contained, you can go back to relating on a more normal, rational basis. As with the Sulker, however, if there are too many recurring problems, and you have to assuage the Sensitive Soul's feelings too often, or if you feel that you are always walking on eggshells with him, the effort of working with him may prove too unrewarding.

The Worrier

The Worrier thinks things are likely to go wrong—and they usually do, often because the Worrier's attitude leads her to deal with others and respond to everyday situations in a way that makes things more difficult. Essentially, the Worrier has the "bean counter" or "batten down the hatches" approach to life, which is fine when a dose of caution is needed. When that attitude is taken too far, however, the Worrier can be a real downer, ready to say no to almost anything because she is so afraid things won't work out.

With one kind of Worrier, a good strategy is to calmly and confidentially present the facts, to counter her gloom-and-doom scenario. Then, if your facts can shift her point of view, the two of you can work together successfully. Another kind of Worrier continually gives "but what if" responses, and you may find her too far advanced on her path of worrying, and too committed to her perspective, to make working with her worth your time and effort. The Worrier may actually feel more comfortable with her pessimistic outlook because she is so accustomed to her negative experience of the world and her own misfortunes.

In many cases, it is best just to work around an unyielding Worrier; use the skills and services she offers, but ignore her worries about what could go wrong. Remember, too, that if you spend too much time around a Worrier, her dismal outlook may start to affect you and make you more negative and pessimistic than usual. When a Worrier begins to pull you into her world, it's time to pull away.

POWER-DRIVEN PROBLEM PEOPLE

Some people are difficult primarily because of the ways in which they use power. They use it to manipulate and control others, sometimes because they have underlying feelings of insecurity. Or sometimes they simply like having power and exercising it over others.

The problem with these people is that they can often take advantage of you or make you feel bad. That's because they don't mind stepping on you as they march toward their goals. In general, you should approach these types cautiously. But you should also understand what makes them tick and learn how to work with them. That way, you can counter their ploys when they try to take advantage of you—and when they exercise their power in order to rise within the organization, you rise, too.

The Pusher

The Pusher wants what he wants when he wants it, and if he can use you to get it, he will. If he can't, he will push you out of the way, especially if he's trying to climb the organizational ladder. If he can use your help, however, he will take it as long as he needs it to advance his own interests. Then he'll push on—and push someone else out of his way.

The Pusher talks a persuasive line to get you to do what you don't want to do—or to do more than you want to do. Then, using various arguments and manipulative strategies, he convinces you to go on doing it.

The way to deal with a Pusher is to not be a pushover. You need to find ways to assertively or diplomatically say no—and say it again and again.

The problem is more difficult when the Pusher is your boss. In that situation, it's hard to say no. But perhaps you can, even if you have to employ manipulative or deceptive strategies yourself. For example, you can develop a very good reason why you can't do something, or you can be plausibly unavailable to be called after hours for extra work. Or maybe you can come up with a creative and acceptable approach, such as sharing work with another person or redesigning work procedures, so that your work becomes more efficient and extra time on the job isn't needed.

Sometimes a direct refusal is the best approach. At other times, it's better to be more diplomatic while still saying no. At still other times, a more strategic approach works best. For example, you appear to give your consent to the Pusher's demand, but then you delay and avoid doing what you don't want to do. (In fact, if you're working for an overworked, distracted Pusher, he may not even realize that you haven't done what he asked.) In the worst case, you may need to fire your Pusher boss and go to work somewhere else.

The Judge

The Judge is a perfectionist critic. She never wants to be wrong. In fact, she believes that she is always right, and she is quick to point out all the ways in which others are wrong. The Judge often comes across as very arrogant and obnoxious, or sometimes as a pedant or snob. But if the Judge is high up in the organization, has a good amount of power (as many do), and actually is right or has a reasonably good idea to offer, then you may want to go along with her "I told you so" attitude. In other words, let her feel right and superior, since she has such a strong need to be perceived in this way. Let her spout off about the best way to do things. All the while, you can be using her skills and services. In fact, if you make the Judge feel good enough, she will often do even more to help with or contribute to your projects.

If you feel, however, that the Judge has become too arrogant and righteous, so that her attitude outweighs her contributions, or if you find her too often or too seriously wrong, then a different strategy may be in order. You might try ignoring her and doing what you want (as long as the Judge is a co-worker to whom you don't have to defer). You might diplomatically point out that there could be considerations that the Judge has overlooked, so that she can be induced to change her opinion without feeling wrong (as when the Judge is your boss).

However, if the Judge is too hard to satisfy or too often wrong, it's best to end your relationship. But do so in a diplomatic way, to avoid suggesting that she has done something wrong: a Judge can hold a grudge for a long time, and she can be vindictive. If you leave the Judge with the impression that she is right, you're less likely to encounter negative repercussions after you have moved on.

The Steamroller

The Steamroller thinks that by rolling over others he will get his way. He may simply be convinced that he is right and eager for everyone around him to see it, too, or he may be acting out of insecurity, overcompensating by being extra aggressive. Whatever the genesis of this style, the Steamroller loves to show off his power and get his own way. In some settings, this style can be quite effective, so you may find the Steamroller at the top of the organizational hierarchy or on his way up. He will browbeat the competition and either rise through his own good work or use his power to get others to do a good job for him—even though he may not have good personal relationships with others and many people probably dislike him. So while it may be lonely at the top for him, the Steamroller doesn't care. Power and success are what motivate him; people are of less concern.

Your best bet is to avoid dealing with the Steamroller as much as you can or to accommodate his demands, say, by giving in on less important issues to calm him down. If you do have to work with or for the Steamroller, listen if he wants to let off steam. Then calmly and surely present your own point of view, but avoid making the Steamroller feel wrong, since this is sure to inspire nothing but a hostile response. Think of your role as that of a peacemaker working toward harmony, and try not to take any attacks on you personally. Bear in mind that this is just the Steamroller's way of being in the world and imagine yourself above the fray.

Sometimes the Steamroller responds well to a dose of humor or even appreciation or praise. This can help him feel acknowledged for his power, while lightening the mood. For example, even if you feel annoyed with the boss who frequently checks up on you, thank him for being so protective of and concerned about you. Or thank the boss who yells at everyone like a drill sergeant with a light comment, such as: "I really appreciate the way you wake us all up in the morning." The gentle mocking may help the Steamroller realize that he is coming on too strongly, without being harsh enough to provoke a defensive response. As a result, he may willingly back off.

In any case, the best strategy with the Steamroller is to get out of the way or use evasive maneuvers to deflect or defuse the attack, adapting your approach to the particular office terrain. In some cases, you may find strength in numbers. If enough people feel undermined by the Steamroller's bullying, than an office meeting to discuss problems and diplomatically suggest changes, so the Steamroller rolls off, might be effective. But be careful. While diplomacy sometimes works, Steamrollers often feel threatened by any challenge to their power—and an open expression of dissatisfaction may be highly provocative, since it may seem like rebellion. Then, if the Steamroller has more power than you, the danger is an office war with you as one of the casualties. So before things erupt or get so bad you end up hiring a lawyer, try to work out your difficulties in other ways. The last thing you want with a Steamroller is a full-scale battle—whether one on one, with others, or with lawyers. In a battle, it's uncertain who will win, and often everyone loses to some degree.

The Control Freak

The Control Freak, another power-driven type who sometimes acts like the Steamroller, wants to be in charge and exercise power but is much more subtle and manipulative about it. The Control Freak uses persuasion and logic rather than open displays of force to get her way. The Control Freak can be quite charming; stand in her way, though, and she can turn into the Steamroller, and you may not even know what hit you.

The Control Freak can be sinister and dangerous because her manipulative style of exercising power affects not just your behavior but also your mind. Not only do you come to do what the Control Freak wants; you also accept her point of view.

Generally speaking, the first step in dealing effectively with the Control Freak is to be aware of her subtle wiles, which come into play when she seeks to manipulate you into doing something you don't think is right or don't feel comfortable doing. She may use an appeal to guilt, suggest that you could do what she wants if you really tried, or give you explanations (which you don't completely accept) about why it will be appropriate for you to act as she insists you should. Some kinds of persuasion are reasonable and legitimate, as when you fear that you don't have the skills to do something, and your boss convinces you that you do have the ability to succeed; what makes the Control Freak's tactics wrong is that she is guiding you to advance her own agenda of gaining control over you.

If you suspect that someone is trying to manipulate or control you, one approach is to pull away as soon as you can: end your work on a project, or seek a transfer into another department. If pulling away isn't an option, then at least disengage yourself emotionally. Remind yourself that you are doing what the Control Freak wants only for now, while you explore other options, and maintain this mental state of detachment. It can also help to share your perceptions with a few people you trust, so that you can have external validation for your feelings and support for your point of view; their support can reinforce your resolve, and others affected by the Control Freak may also choose to distance themselves and disengage.

Occasionally, a confrontation may clear the air: you can let the Control Freak know that you know what she is up to, and you can try to lay the foundation for a more egalitarian relationship. Often, however, a confrontational approach won't work because the Control Freak's actions are usually so quietly manipulative that they're hard to call, and her response is likely to be denial: "You're just imagining this." The best approach may be to leave or, if you can't, to use the same manipulative strategies that she does. Let the Control Freak think you're still playing her game; all the while, you'll be turning her own tactics against her and eluding her control.

RULE MINDERS, MAKERS, BENDERS, AND BREAKERS

The people in this group are difficult because of the way in which they deal with rules. They're too rigid, or they tend to ignore the rules and make their own, or they just do nothing. Wherever these types are found, they can be annoying and frustrating to work with. You generally need to accept their quirks, so that they bother you less. Sometimes you can get them to make adjustments, or you can make some yourself—an approach of fine-tuning the rules, yours or theirs, for a better fit.

The Clock Watcher

The Clock Watcher doesn't like or feel committed to her job, or she feels underpaid, and so she doesn't want to work more than she has to. There are likely to be more Clock Watchers in larger organizations, where people can more easily get away with this kind of behavior; in some organizations, whole divisions or departments are made up of Clock Watchers. Typically, the Clock Watcher doesn't become truly difficult to work with until there is pressure to perform at a rate faster than the usual one. At that point, problems may develop as the Clock Watcher resists changing and doing more.

A good way to deal with the Clock Watcher on a day-to-day basis, if she is otherwise doing a good job, is to try to work around her schedule and not introduce pressure for major changes, which might lead her to become defensive and resentful. If you are the Clock Watcher's co-worker or underling, you don't have the power to do much to change her behavior. If you are the Clock Watcher's boss, and if her behavior is becoming a serious problem, a good approach might be to have a talk with her and find out why she is behaving in this way. Since the Clock Watcher's behavior is shaped by the rules, consider ways of changing them so that you are both more comfortable. For example, you might offer an increase in pay in return for measurably improved performance, or, if there is an important deadline, you might explain the situation so that the Clock Watcher understands the need to work longer hours for a time. The Clock Watcher is usually one of the least difficult people to work with if you can reach an understanding and make a mutually agreeable arrangement about the rules.

The By-the-Booker

The By-the-Booker can be infuriatingly rigid. He is most likely to be found in more structured settings (government, law enforcement, school systems, the military), where it's important to follow the rules; he is less commonly found in settings where human relationships and creativity are primary values.

If your boss is a By-the-Booker, the best way to deal with him is to conform to his expectations as well as you can. Organize the room or write the memos exactly the way he likes; that way, you'll have more peace and harmony. If you have a By-the-Booker co-worker, again, go along with his expectations as best you can, and defer to his preferences in matters of little importance to you. In matters of greater importance to you, one strategy is to make a logical and reasonable case for your way of doing things, since the By-the-Booker tends to respond to logic and rules. If he won't budge, try to work around him.

If you have a By-the-Booker employee, usually you just have to be very precise about what you want done, and he will do it; things will generally be fine if you don't expect much creativity or initiative, and if you don't leave much to his discretion. If it does become necessary for the By-the-Booker to take more initiative, spend some time discussing alternative scenarios and possibilities with him, so that he has some guidelines for what to do in various situations. He should then feel more comfortable about adapting the rules to fit the circumstances.

The Tit-for-Tatter

Most people hope for a show of appreciation, and even some reciprocation, when they do something to help others, especially if they do more than expected or put in volunteer time and effort on a project. The Tit-for-Tatter is difficult because she carefully keeps track of assistance or favors that she gives to others, usually her co-workers, and then expects a payback and feels resentful if she doesn't get one. Sometimes the Tit-for-Tatter even puts in extra work on a project in order to make this kind of claim on others. As a result, her wish to be recognized or rewarded for a good deed well done can be irritating and annoying; instead of appreciating her, others wish that she would just shut up or go away.

The most pragmatic approach to working with the Tit-for-Tatter is not to get drawn into her cycle of stepped-up assistance and demands for payback. It may be all right at first to accept a limited amount of assistance if you need her aid (and usually the Tit-for-Tatter will have some valuable skills), and it may be fine to show your appreciation by doing something for her in return. But don't rely on the Tit-for-Tatter too often, and don't let yourself become too dependent on her. Realize, too, that any attempt to discuss her "helping" behavior with her is unlikely to be effective, since the Tit-for-Tatter will probably deny any intentions beyond offering assistance.

The Do-It-My-Wayer

The Do-It-My-Wayer thinks he knows the best way to get things done. Unlike the Judge, however, he isn't motivated by the desire to wield power or criticize others; rather, the Do-It-My-Wayer is simply comfortable with how he has always done things. He is set in his ways.

His approach may be harmless or even effective in a stable, stodgy organization. However, because this approach often stifles creativity and discourages change, it may become less effective as time goes on and the organization needs to keep up with the times.

If the Do-It-My-Wayer is in a position of power, getting him to change may be difficult. The best strategy may be to follow his lead most of the time while looking for opportunities to do tasks more productively in newer, better ways (as long as they don't interfere with the habits of the Do-It-My-Wayer). Then, after you have made successful use of a newer, better way, patiently and tactfully try to introduce the Do-It-My-Wayer to that approach. If he still can't be moved, it may be time for you to do a cost-benefits analysis of your situation (see Chapter 2, "How Do You Know When It's Time to Go?"). If the Do-It-My-Wayer is your co-worker or your employee, you can be more assertive in encouraging him to consider alternatives. In either case, recognize that habit or fear is usually the basis of the Do-It-My-Wayer's commitment to his own way of doing things. If you can show him a better way and help him be comfortable trying another approach, you may be able to promote change.

The Naysayer

The Naysayer, like the By-the-Booker, resists change. Whereas a By-the-Booker will usually resist quietly, or passively, the Naysayer is quite vocal and finds flaws in every new idea. Often the Naysayer is in a position of power, as a gatekeeper, and has the ability to block or slow progress; sometimes she even has the official function of exercising caution or maintaining a bottom-line orientation. In some cases, however, she takes on the Naysayer role because the prospect of change makes her nervous.

The Naysayer can be maddening, but her ideas may also be valuable: she can alert you to potential pitfalls, and so you can avert problems. Therefore, a good way to deal with the Naysayer and her negativity is to recognize her positive contributions and address the particular concerns she raises. Then, if you can reassure the Naysayer with facts and logic, you can help her feel more comfortable, and her resistance will fade.

If this strategy doesn't work, and if the Naysayer's negative attitude is keeping a good project from moving forward, seek to overcome her negative attitude. Point out that her negative reaction to every suggestion is causing you to wonder whether she is open to any alternatives at all. If she is receptive, then ask for her suggestions, and try to incorporate them into your plans. Because the Naysayer tends to have a deep fear of failure, she needs reassurance that you are prepared to deal with problems that arise. If you show that you're willing to take responsibility yourself, the Naysayer's resistance may diminish, since she will be absolved in advance of any possible blame.

Be aware, however, that Naysayers, like By-the-Bookers, are common in some organizations, where naysaying is part of the organizational culture. When you're working in this kind of organization, you have to try harder and longer to get new ideas adopted. If you feel that implementing a new idea or project is worth the extra effort, try to counteract the Naysayers by lining up all the support you can get, in the form of facts and personal endorsements. But if the naysaying culture proves too frustrating, time-consuming, or hopeless, cut your losses and move on: find someone else, in another setting, to say yes to your good ideas.

The Super-Agreeable Flake

Given his affable manner, the Super-Agreeable Flake seems quite nice and pleasant, not difficult at all. In his apparent eagerness to help, he may superficially resemble the Tit-for-Tatter. Instead of taking the initiative, however, he generally waits for someone else to ask him to do something, and he agrees to do it—but then he never follows through, or he does, but only after many delays, although he is quick to offer excuses as well as assurances that next time he will be happy to help.

Whether the Agreeable Flake is your boss, your employee, or your co-worker, the best strategy for dealing with him is to weigh the benefits of working with him against the costs of his unreliability. If you decide to continue working with him, a good first step is to let him know that you want to hear the truth from him about what he is actually able to do, whether that means his delivering on a promised raise or promotion (if he's your boss) or his carrying out a task that he has agreed to perform (if he's your employee or co-worker). Stress that what concerns you is not whether he agrees to do something, but whether he follows through after having made such an agreement. Tell him that what matters most to you is that your working relationship be one of openness, honesty, and trust. Before he is able to tell you the truth, you may have to reassure him several times, since he may be afraid to say no and thus not seem agreeable.

If the Super-Agreeable Flake is able to make this change, the problem will disappear. You'll know where he really stands, and you will no longer feel the letdown that used to come from his failure to follow through. He may no longer be super-agreeable, but he won't be a flake, either. If you should discover, though, that he has simply agreed one more time but doesn't follow through on this change in behavior, then you will have two choices: you can accept his eager-to-be-agreeable but haphazard style, or you can cut the cord.

The Procrastinator

The Procrastinator is most likely to be found in an organization where delays and careful consideration are a way of life. In a way, the Procrastinator is a cousin to the Super-Agreeable Flake, since she doesn't follow through, either. The big difference is that the Procrastinator doesn't make the eager, helpful promises that the Super-Agreeable Flake does. Instead, she simply waits to take action, sometimes letting you know that an outcome is uncertain or that there will be a delay. And then you wait, and you wait—and maybe the Procrastinator eventually does come through, especially when a deadline looms and she makes that final "beat the clock" sprint.

A common reason why the Procrastinator puts things off is that she wants to be perfect or believes that she shouldn't ask for help. Another reason, particularly in a large organization, is that the Procrastinator is afraid of making a decision. Wherever she is in the organization, she wants to be sure that others approve, and she wants to make sure that she has the necessary input and approval. Rather than take the initiative to get the needed feedback, however, she hesitates and delays.

If you are frustrated by the Procrastinator's inaction, a good strategy is to talk with her about the reasons for the delay. Then, according to the reasons she gives, you can offer to take some action to help her move forward: maybe you can find some information she needs, or you can offer your reassurance that the action she is considering will be fine. If the Procrastinator is willing, you may also help her brainstorm ways of solving the problem and getting things moving again.

OTHER DIFFICULT TYPES

The difficult types described up this point represent a broad sampling of the most common varieties. But it's only a sampling; you may find other types. We'll look at three more here.

The Sniping Sneak

The Sniping Sneak tries to cut others down with behind-the-scenes machinations, wounding remarks, and veiled shows of aggression. He sometimes conceals his criticisms with humor, but his aim has not changed: to undermine others and their work.

Sometimes the Sneak tries to take credit for your work. If he can't do that, he may try to sabotage it rather than let you get the credit. He commonly thinks that his behavior is fully justified, telling himself that others have done something wrong, and he is the secret avenger setting things right. He may also justify his tactics as a way of rising to the top in the corporate game of office politics: if he can keep from getting caught, make himself look good, and make others who are in his way look bad, why not? The Sneak is generally found toward the middle or bottom of the corporate hierarchy or professional career ladder; after all, if one has power, there is no need for sniping or sneaking.

Whatever the Sneak's hierarchical level or particular modus operandi, if you are no longer willing to dodge or live with his sniping attacks, the first step is to bring them out in the open. This is sometimes done effectively in the presence of others, where the Sneak can't deny what he has done or is trying to do. For example, if the Sneak has made a sarcastic remark to put you down at a meeting, or if he is claiming credit for a project you originally proposed, you can say, without getting emotional, "Was that meant as a put-down?" or "You must have forgotten that I raised this idea several weeks ago."

If the Sneak then denies your claim, present your evidence calmly and matter-of-factly. If you do this repeatedly, the Sneak will realize that you're on to him, and he'll seek another target.

In other circumstances, it may be better to quietly approach the Sneak alone, and let him know that you know what he's doing. Give him a chance both to save face and to stop doing what he is doing. This more personal, diplomatic approach is also a way to avoid open warfare, and it may allow you to learn the underlying reasons why the Sneak is targeting you; it can be a way to make peace and clear the air. For example, you might arrange a meeting with the Sneak to discuss what you perceive as a problem; then, at your meeting, you describe an incident and how you felt: "Was the remark you made at yesterday's meeting meant as a put-down?" If you are dealing with a stealthier attack—for example, if the Sneak has been stealing your sales leads—let him see that you know. Then, if he tries to deny it, present your evidence. Keep your cool, so he doesn't feel you are aggressively attacking him. If he does, he may escalate the situation. Take the attitude that you want to work out rules and guidelines for the future.

Once you've blown the Sneak's cover, he is likely to pull back, either because you have resolved the underlying problem or because he fears the consequences if he strikes and is caught again. He'll have to stop his attacks or openly justify them.

The Space Case

The Space Case inhabits her own little world. When she's tuned in to collective reality, she can be very skilled and productive, but when she's off in her world of ideas, it may be difficult to get her to work effectively on day-to-day projects or meet tight deadlines. She becomes forgetful, doesn't follow through, procrastinates, doesn't pay attention, and otherwise lacks focus because her interest and attention are elsewhere.

The basic strategy in dealing with the Space Case is to help her get regrounded and refocused so that she can perform well in a timely manner. For example, give her a clear list of tasks to do, and follow up to see that she is doing them and making deadlines. Send her short, to-the-point memos, and follow up to see that she has read and is acting on them.

Whenever you can, give the Space Case projects on which she can work independently, on her own schedule. The value of this approach is that it encourages the Space Case to perform effectively while it gives her extra space to follow her own rhythms.

The Gossip

The Gossip is usually found toward the bottom or middle of the organization, since those at the top are less likely to talk and spread rumors. The Gossip can seem amusing and entertaining. Who doesn't enjoy hearing the scoop? But when the Gossip talks too much or undermines you and the organization, he can become a serious problem. He may waste others' time and reduce productivity, and he may be spreading trade secrets, divulging personal details about others, or disseminating incorrect or damaging information. Sometimes his tales, whether factual or not, can also contribute to dissension within a work group, as when one person hears that another person is spreading negative information about him.

One approach to the Gossip is simply not to listen: say you're busy and don't want to hear what he has to say. Another approach is to confront the Gossip by saying that you know he is spreading stories. Even if he denies it (a common response), you can say that you want the rumormongering to stop, regardless of who is responsible. By making this statement, you put the Gossip on notice that you suspect him. If he is the party responsible for the rumors, he is likely to stop circulating them. If he simply tries to be more discreet, however, and the rumors continue, confront him again. This will show him that the odds of getting caught are mounting, and that if he does get caught again, he is likely to face more severe consequences in the future—whether from you or from others in the organization.

ASSESSING YOUR ORGANIZATION

Now that you have familiarized yourself with the various types of difficult people you might encounter in a work situation, take a moment to reflect on your own organization. Use Worksheets 10 and 11 to help you begin to strategize steps you might take in working with the difficult people in your company.

WORKSHEET 10

Dealing with Difficult People in My Organization

Name of difficult person

_____

Type of difficult person

_____

_____

_____

What's bothering him or her?

_____

_____

_____

_____

What can I do to help?

_____

_____

_____

_____

What can the organization do to help?

_____

_____

_____

_____

_____

_____

WORKSHEET 11

Dealing with a Difficult Individual

If you repeatedly have difficulties with a particular person, it is a good idea to document the problems. Such a record can be useful as a reference in a discussion and is generally required to justify taking action, such as suspending or terminating that person's employment. After filling the chart below, use the guide that follows to help you think about possible strategies and choose what you want to do.

Name of difficult person

_____

Overall nature of difficulties

_____

_____

Nature of problem   **Date of incident**

_____

What happened

_____

_____

What I did to respond

_____

_____

What others did to respond

_____

_____

Strategies/comments

_____

_____

_____

Dealing with a Difficult Individual

Deciding What to Do

Step 1 A Guided Reflection

First get very relaxed in a quiet place. Then, close your eyes and imagine yourself in a large theater with a big screen. Imagine that you are a director watching a film, which you can either just watch or change at any time. Now, on the screen see your office and the difficult person with whom you are having problems.

Notice that person working, interacting with others and with you.

• Pay attention to the times when problems arise.

• Notice what happens before the person becomes difficult.

• Observe what triggers an incident involving difficult behavior.

Then, think about what you can do. Imagine yourself using different intervention techniques to deal with the problem and change future outcomes, and observe what happens. Ask yourself a series of "what if" questions, and notice how the person on the screen responds. For example, you might ask:

• What if I talk to the person about the problem?

• What if I ask an associate to talk to the person about the problem?

• What if I avoid the person who is being difficult?

• What if I assign the person to another work group?

Finally, decide which of the endings you want to try on your film. In your still relaxed state, reflect on the various "what if" questions you have asked and the results. Then, ask yourself which result you liked best. Which "what if" scenario would you like to try in real life?

WORKSHEET 11 (CONT'D)

Dealing with a Difficult Individual

Deciding What to Do

Step 2 Writing Up the Results

Now take some time to record in writing what you have experienced. Note what you asked, what the results were, and what you decided to do. Then, later, write down what you actually did and what happened. Over time as you repeat this exercise, you will find yourself becoming more sensitive to the difficult people you deal with and deciding on the best approaches for dealing with the problem. Use the following worksheet to help you in writing down your results.

Name of difficult person

_____

Possible approaches ("what if" possibilities)

_____

_____

Possible results (what I imagined)

_____

_____

Preferred choice

_____

_____

What I actually did

_____

_____

What happened in response

_____

_____

CHAPTER 6

Choosing an Appropriate Conflict Style

You can approach any conflict in a number of ways:

- You can be competitive or confrontational and use your power to get what you want.

- You can collaborate on a resolution by sharing your interests and concerns with others involved in the conflict.

- You can avoid the conflict by walking away from it, or you can put off dealing with it.

- You can accommodate the wishes of others involved in the conflict by doing what they want.

- You can compromise by giving up a little of what you want in return for others' giving up a little of what they want.

You can also use a combination of these approaches. The one you choose will depend on the situation, your preferred way of handling conflict, the way in which other parties prefer to handle conflict, your respective resources, how important the situation is, how much time there is to find a resolution, and many other factors. There is no one right approach, but if you are aware that there are various specific styles of handling conflict, and if you have some knowledge of the circumstances in which each style is most likely to be effective, you can draw as necessary on these styles. This chapter discusses five styles of handling conflict, shows you how to identify your own preferred style and the styles of others, and offers guidance for deciding which style to use in different situations.

THE FIVE CONFLICT STYLES

The five major styles of handling conflict that are discussed in this chapter have been widely described and used by researchers, educators, human resource professionals, trainers, and others who have based their work on a system originally conceptualized by Kenneth W. Thomas and Ralph H. Kilmann. Their system is embodied in the *Thomas–Kilmann Conflict Mode Instrument,* which they developed in the early 1970s. (The term *mode* in the instrument's title is also an acronym for "management of differences exercise.") Much of the information in this chapter is drawn from using that instrument.

Thomas and Kilmann's five conflict styles reflect ways of reacting to a conflict or a difficult situation along one of two axes: the degree to which you address your own concerns (by acting either assertively or unassertively), and the degree to which you address others' concerns (by acting either cooperatively or uncooperatively). When these two axes are combined, they form a grid of four cells with one central cell, yielding five different conflict styles: *Competing, Collaborating, Avoiding, Accommodating,* and *Compromising.* These styles are shown in Figure 4.

You can use Figure 4 to identify your own or anyone else's style of handling conflict. As the figure shows, if your approach tends to be both assertive and uncooperative, then you are more likely to use the Competing style. If your approach tends to be both assertive and cooperative, then you are more likely to use the Collaborating style. If your approach tends to be both unassertive and uncooperative, then you are more likely to use the Avoiding style. If your approach tends to be both unassertive and cooperative, then you are more likely to use the Accommodating style. And if your approach is somewhere in between being assertive and being unassertive, and in between being cooperative and being uncooperative, then you are more likely to use the Compromising style.

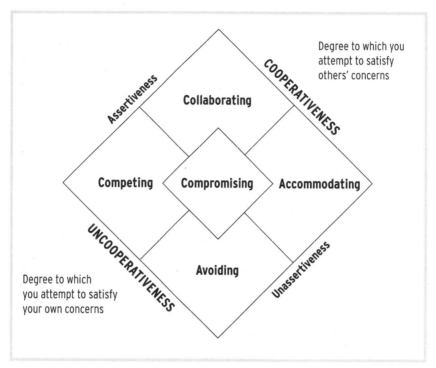

Figure 4   FIVE STYLES OF HANDLING CONFLICT

The style you identify may be the one that you normally use, or it may be one that you use in particular circumstances, or with certain people. For example, if you have a low-status position in a large organization, you may be more apt to respond with the Competing style if you have a dispute with someone at the same level as yours; in a dispute with your boss, however, where you have less power, you may be more likely to respond with the Accommodating style, even if you feel that you are right. As a supervisor, you may adopt the Competing style with someone who reports to you; if a dispute develops with another supervisor, however, you may be more likely to adopt the Collaborating style, taking the time to discuss the problem and share your ideas about what to do; and if you have a conflict with your own boss, you may react with the Accommodating style, or perhaps even with the Avoiding style as you gather more facts to support your position.

Competing

The Competing style of handling conflict involves being forceful and confrontational in seeking to get what you want, irrespective of how others feel. It also includes being manipulative, persuasive, argumentative, and combative in getting people to go along with your point of view. Sometimes, if you have the benefit of a higher position, it can include pulling rank and using your power to win your objective.

If you have the power to support this approach, it can be an effective, efficient style to use—say, to push a project through quickly when there has been continual conflict among those with less power about how to carry out the project. The downside is that you may obtain your objective in the short term but then experience long-term fallout because there is still dissension, even though it may not be openly expressed in the face of superior force. This is what happened when Vicki used her power as the head of a marketing team at a major financial institution.

Competition Depletes Team Commitment

Vicki liked running the team with strong, tight leadership, with herself firmly in control, although this approach squelched the group's creativity. From time to time, members of the team would come up with ideas about additional projects the group could do or suggest alternative ads or marketing campaigns, but generally Vicki shot down any such proposals or avoided acting on them by taking them to management for further discussion and approval. So little changed. While a few frustrated team members dropped out and went to other companies, the remaining marketing team members usually went along with whatever Vicki wanted.

Then, a conflict erupted over designing a new brochure for the company. A recently hired copywriter, Franklin, had a number of ideas for giving the company a higher profile, including a new logo and slogan, since the company was losing market share in an increasingly competitive business environment. As part of this effort, Franklin worked on designing a brochure and ad campaign that could be used to promote the company. Soon, though, friction developed between Vicki's directive style and Franklin's own forceful style. For about a month, Vicki and Franklin went back and forth, writing and rewriting the brochure and ads and offering different design possibilities. Finally, Franklin took his vision for the brochure and for how the team could create an even better ad campaign to the whole team. One by one he spoke to the other team members, until he got their agreement. They liked what he had done, and they agreed to support Franklin's ideas at their next regular team meeting.

For a time, the discussion about Franklin's proposed campaign seemed to go well. Franklin reported that he had the group's support for his last rewrite and redesign, and as the discussion about the brochure and ads he had designed concluded, everything seemed to be on track. But then Vicki began speaking forcefully about how she already had the company's agreement on the present campaign, and she contended that it didn't make sense to present a new vision now. To Franklin's argument that his approach would be better and would help give the company a new look to revitalize its declining market share, Vicki responded that his efforts would just create confusion—and might even lead to the company's dissatisfaction with the team itself. Finally, Vicki played her trump card, informing Franklin that, being the new person on the team, he didn't understand the politics of dealing with the company's management team. Furthermore, she said, as the marketing team leader she was responsible for making the final decisions about what the team did. It was her way of telling Franklin "I'm in charge."

Vicki's approach worked, or so it seemed. The other team members quickly backed down from supporting Franklin's ideas to side with Vicki, and Vicki got what she wanted—continued control over the group. But while she won this battle, in the long run she lost the war because the confrontation marked the beginning of a process of demoralizing and undermining the whole team. Over the next few weeks, Franklin pulled back from doing anything more than his job absolutely required, while others in the group began to reassess whether they wanted to remain on the team. Several members quit to join other companies, and Franklin began looking around for opportunities he could pursue once he put in a few more months with the company to build up his resume. While the team did continue, it became a far less effective group, which eventually led Vicki's own supervisor to criticize her leadership of the team and reassign her to a less desirable position in the company doing more marketing research rather than remaining on the management track.

Vicki's conflict style may have helped her win her immediate objective, but it wasn't the best approach in the long run. By turning her leadership into a win–lose battle with Franklin, Vicki managed to impose her own will, but she also undermined the long-term strength of the group, as well as her own position in the company.

Because the Competing style involves a power play to resolve a conflict, consider not only whether you actually have the strength to win but also whether you really want to win in this way. How important is this particular issue or battle to you? How will it affect you in the future? Will it contribute to your long-term goals? Or will you prevail in this instance but undermine your future objectives and goals, thereby winning the battle but losing the war?

Such considerations are important when you use this style, since you are generally seeking to satisfy your concerns at the expense of others. Whether it means forcefully arguing your point of view, giving orders, or pulling rank, you are using your power to get others to do things your way. Therefore, even if you have the power to use the Competing style, it is not always the best one to use, given the potential for negative reactions down the line.

If you don't have the institutional power to adopt the Competing style, then it is not the one to use. If you do have the power to use it, the Competing style can be effective in the following situations:

- When you have the authority to make a decision, know that your strategy or approach, although perhaps not popular, is the right one (a judgment borne out by the facts and by input from others), and feel that it is crucial to implement this strategy or approach now

- When you have a great deal at stake in a decision or in the result of a project and are committed to making sure it produces a particular outcome

- When a group discussion has bogged down and you feel that decisive leadership is needed to break the impasse and move the group

- When there is an emergency and someone has to make a quick decision and take action right away

- When you feel that you have run out of alternatives, are willing to make an all-or-nothing effort to gain your objective, and are ready to leave if your approach doesn't work (this, essentially, is a "do it my way or I resign" ploy)

Collaborating

The Collaborating style of handling conflict takes longer than the other styles, since it involves a real commitment to discussing and trying to understand the issues. It includes openly airing and addressing everyone's concerns and listening to everyone's goals, opinions, and needs. It also requires some skills in expression and articulation, and so it isn't the easiest style to master. But if you and others have the time, and if the issue is an important or complex one to which this style is suited, the Collaborating style can lead to a win-win solution. (Of course, you won't want to invest the time and effort needed in the Collaborating style to handle everyday conflicts, such as small disputes about late deliveries or who owes what to whom.)

With the Collaborating style, unspoken and sometimes even unconscious concerns may be uncovered so that the true, deep-seated conflict can then be resolved. Consider, for example, the employee who, after being a superior performer for some time, begins to arrive at the office late or starts making mistakes. Your initial reaction may be to blame some external problem: tensions at home, or drinking too much. But a closer look, one that uses the Collaborating style, may reveal that the employee's declining performance reflects disappointment at having been passed over for promotion, or feelings of not being appreciated for work well done. The employee, not feeling free to discuss the real source of dissatisfaction, disconnects from work. If the real, deep-seated issue is never confronted, this employee could leave—or stay while expressing negative feelings indirectly (for example, by making personal use of office supplies and facilities). But if the employee's actual feelings and needs can be drawn out and addressed through a Collaborating approach to the problem of declining performance, then the organization stands to retain a valued worker. For example, this might have been a good approach for Joan and David.

Lack of Collaboration
Causes Conflict

Joan and David were newly appointed department heads in a major retail chain. Each was responsible for managing a different group of salespeople. While the two groups were in charge of different departments with different merchandise in the store, sometimes they worked on joint projects, such as holiday parties and storewide sale days.

However, it wasn't always clear which group or department leader was heading up a particular project. As a result, there was often confusion about who was doing what, and sometimes follow-through and support for different projects fell through the cracks. At times, the salespeople weren't sure what to do or blamed others when tasks went undone or were done incorrectly.

Joan and David griped to others as well as to each other about the problems in coordinating their groups. Sometimes they felt angry with each other, feeling that the other person wasn't doing his or her job or was unfairly taking the credit. Most of the time they kept their feelings concealed, since the culture of the store dictated that they stay cool and professional and not display emotion. But sometimes their feelings boiled over into displays of anger, and often there was a lot of tension between them, which also affected their staff. This was an ideal situation for the use of collaboration. Joan and David had an ongoing relationship, and the problem was a complex one, not a candidate for a quick and easy solution. Moreover, it was important that the problem be resolved quickly, before it undermined their effectiveness and that of the salespeople under their direction.

Joan and David would do well to devote some time to examining their particular areas of conflict, such as the confusion over which group they supervised was supposed to do what. Then, they could work out specific guidelines for how all parties should work together, clarifying task assignments, lines of authority, and time lines for action. As department heads, both Joan and David had the power to develop such guidelines and implement them, and such a collaborative effort not only would help guide their groups but would help them overcome their tension in dealing with each other. The process of collaborating would help them air their issues and the unexpressed emotions that had sprung up as a barrier between them. So the process itself would be healing, and it would help them achieve their mutual desired result of a smoother, more effective and efficient operation.

In general, the Collaborating style is effective in the following situations (and is sometimes the only approach that will provide a long-term solution):

- When you and other parties consider the issue very important and are willing to take the time to work out a mutually satisfying resolution

- When you and other parties have a close, continuing, or interdependent relationship and expect it to continue

- When the difficulties are complicated or of long standing

- When, despite the positions or interests that are openly expressed, the actual root of the conflict is an unexpressed desire or need

- When you and other parties have the skills to express your concerns effectively and listen to one another

- When you and the other parties are at a similar level of organizational power or are willing to work together in a spirit of equality, setting aside power differences in the interest of a fair, mutually satisfying resolution

- When you and other parties are willing to set aside anger, hostility, or bitterness in the interest of working thoughtfully and amicably toward a resolution (even if you may initially have to work through such feelings)

Avoiding

In many ways, the Avoiding style of handling conflict is the opposite of the Competing style. Instead of responding with force and power, you retreat and withdraw. You don't assert yourself, and you don't cooperate or engage in any way—at least for now. Iris used this approach in the following example.

Avoiding Leads to Win-Win Result

Iris was in charge of organizing a community seminar program for her company, which was designed to increase the company's profile in the community. The company assigned individuals from different divisions to be part of the effort. The project initially didn't have much support among the participants assigned to it because they saw it as pro bono work that added extra hours and took them away from their regular work—in some cases, work that brought in bonuses and commissions. Thus, they felt little motivation to participate, and Iris initially got little cooperation or support from them.

So she worked mostly on her own to make arrangements for meeting facilities and for several local speakers and celebrities to participate in the program. Iris felt that doing a good job in staging this event might help her gain recognition and advancement in the company. Thus, although she was disappointed by the lack of support from others, she carried on and did what needed to be done.

After she had made all the arrangements, once the speakers had been confirmed and the press had expressed interest, the other employees assigned to the project suddenly became interested. At a meeting a week before the event to discuss final arrangements, several now forcefully expressed their opinions. One person volunteered to be the master of ceremonies, and the group offered ideas on how to set up the room.

But as the project members spoke with growing enthusiasm about how they wanted to run the event, Iris began to feel angry. Now that she had done most of the work to put on a successful event, she was being pushed out of her leadership role. After leaving her to do all the planning and make all the arrangements, the other project members now wanted to take over the event and score the glory. But rather than expressing her feelings, Iris held back, deciding that it was best to let the others run with the event and make it successful. Otherwise she felt she not only risked undermining the event, but she could poison her relationships with these co-workers and with her supervisors who had assigned her to the project. At the same time, she reasoned that if the event were successful, she could at least take the credit for acting as the coordinator of the group that had made it a success. As a result, she withdrew from further leadership of the event and let the others on the committee take over.

The event was, in fact, very successful. The project members acknowledged Iris at the event by giving her a small gift as a token of their appreciation. So by using an Avoiding strategy, even though it went against her natural inclinations since she was so angry, Iris pursued an approach that turned into a win–win result for all.

Some may consider use of the Avoiding style to be a form of running away or evading the issue, but there are times when that is the best thing to do—by withdrawing, retreating, delaying, or using other forms of disengagement, including those that follow:

- Changing the subject, or dropping it

- Not giving your opinion

- Leaving the room

- Not responding to a phone call, or not returning it

- Taking a day off, or going on a vacation

- Delaying your response to a letter, or not responding at all

- Dropping a troubled project and starting a new one

Used appropriately, the Avoiding style can be very effective, particularly in the following circumstances:

- When you want to cut your losses

- When you don't think you can win, no matter what you do

- When you don't feel that the issue is important enough to warrant your engagement

- When you have little power at your disposal, or when you feel that others involved in the situation have more power, more allies, or more support from higher-ups

- When you want some time to prepare or get more information or resources

- When you are too busy or too stressed to deal with the situation right away

- When you feel that you are in the wrong

- When proceeding would mean working with a difficult person, whereas withdrawing would free you to do something else

- When you can delay a decision, and you choose to do so because you are unsure about what to do

- When you are very tense or angry or sense that others are, and you want things to calm down

- When you feel that the situation is too complex for you to take on at the moment, and that you don't have the ability to handle it successfully

- When you feel that others are in a better position to deal with the situation, and you choose to defer to them

- When you feel that trying to resolve the situation openly could make things worse, and you hope that the situation can resolve itself

Accommodating

The Accommodating style of handling conflict is the approach of going along with others and doing what they want. Whatever your reason for using this style, you put your own concerns and interests on the back burner. When you acquiesce to others' wishes, you may have to put off resolving a situation in a way that is satisfying to you, just as you do when you use the Avoiding style. But this kind of delay is quite different from the delay involved in the Avoiding style, since here you are going along with what others want instead of doing nothing, and you are letting others shape your response instead of choosing for yourself not to engage with the situation.

Sometimes deferring to the interests of others is the ideal approach, as when doing so will win you their support in the future; thus an accommodation in one situation becomes a gain in another. Using the Accommodating style can also be effective if you are in a low-status position, since being helpful and cooperative and being a good team player are qualities that can serve you in getting ahead. Therefore, deferring to others can be a good strategy for advancement, even if it feels uncomfortable to play along (say, when you disagree with some of the things you are asked to do). At a later time, when conditions are more favorable, you can use another approach. As the following example shows, this is what Jennifer did.

Taking the High Road by Accommodating

Jennifer had recently taken a job as a marketing assistant at a health club that was one of a chain of such clubs. One of her duties was preparing letters and newsletters for prospective customers. After she had been at the company for about a month, she wrote an article for a newsletter of which she felt particularly proud. In the article, she described a new diet program she felt would appeal to anyone. She shared her own experiences in losing weight on the program, feeling that her account would be especially persuasive. Just as she was about to send the newsletter out to the press and to about 6,000 neighborhood prospects, several directors from the main office of the company came to visit. When one of the directors, Thomas, saw the newsletter, he thought it would be a good idea for the message to come from him directly. And so Thomas wrote his own letter to prospective customers, replacing the letter Jennifer had written, and telling Jennifer he would like her to publish his version. The next day, Thomas and the other directors flew off to visit another health club in the chain.

Jennifer was very upset by Thomas's handling of the situation, feeling humiliated and demeaned by the way he had substituted his letter for hers. Worse, his letter lacked her personal touch, which she felt would be appealing to others with diet problems.

But what should she do? Try to argue it out with Thomas and convince him to use her approach? She felt she couldn't do that since she was new, the directors would think of her as a difficult upstart, and they could overrule her anyway. Neither was taking out Thomas's letter and printing her own in the newsletter an option, since Thomas and the directors could readily find out what she had done and probably would be angry that she had defied an order. So she could easily be fired, she felt, if she did that. She also didn't want to quit her job over the issue, since otherwise she liked the work. So confronting and avoiding were not options. And there was no way to discuss the matter since the directors were gone, and there was no possibility of compromise. Thomas's letter would either be printed or not; Jennifer had been granted no editorial discretion.

Thus, the only real alternative seemed to be accommodation. For a time Jennifer was very upset, feeling demeaned, humiliated, disappointed, and even a little depressed about giving in. But in the end she became reconciled to the idea of going along with what Thomas wanted and overcoming her negative feelings. It was more important to her to keep her job and work to advance in the organization than to win, especially since she was a newcomer not only in the company but in the field. Later, when she had more experience in the field and more power in the organization, she might be able to use another approach should a similar situation occur.

The Accommodating style is often the best one to use in the following circumstances:

- When you can't win, because you have little power in the situation

- When others have especially strong feelings about doing something in a particular way

- When you feel it's most important that everyone get along

- When the outcome of the situation isn't important to you or when the issue is more important to others than it is to you

- When you realize that your own position is weaker or that your opinion is wrong, and that the other person has a stronger position or is right

- When you feel that it may be best to let others learn from any mistakes that may result from their doing things their way

Compromising

The Compromising style of handling conflict is the middle way. You give up a little of what you each want, others give up a little of what they want, and you all end up with some of what you want. Sometimes you split the difference; sometimes you make exchanges and concessions in the course of bargaining, to come up with a mutually acceptable solution. For example, say that you and someone else are competing for a job that offers not just a desirable title and a better office but also the opportunity to attend high-level meetings and travel to branch offices. One of you is something of a loner and is more interested in the title and the better office; the other person is more attracted by the travel and the meetings. In this case, a compromise might split the position into two different functions with two different titles. (See "Compromise Versus Collaboration," on page 113, for more information about developing a compromise and for information about how compromise differs from collaboration.)

In many cases, finding a compromise involves bargaining back and forth about different possibilities until a resolution is reached. Or one party can suggest a compromise by taking into consideration what both parties want and offering a solution that satisfies both.

Compromising Opens Up
Middle Ground

Sam hired Jim, a consultant and speaker, to put on a training program for Sam's company. He paid Jim one-third up front, with the rest to come after Jim put on the program. Then, Sam engaged in an extensive period of bargaining back and forth with Jim about exactly what he wanted. He asked Jim to extend the program from four to six hours by adding an additional morning session. Jim was glad to add the extra session but indicated that the cost would be increased, and Sam agreed, promising to put in a requisition for the extra money.

However, when Jim actually put on the program, Sam got some early feedback from his employees that they didn't like the program. They felt that Jim was covering information they already knew and that he didn't fully understand their concerns. They felt he was just giving them very general motivational and inspirational material, when what they really wanted was a more brass-tacks presentation on how to handle day-to-day customer service topics.

Jim was surprised when Sam gave him the grim report, saying that he had prepared exactly what Sam had led him to believe the employees wanted. Sam, in turn, blamed Jim for not taking the time to interview the employees and learn more about their needs. Jim felt that Sam should have told him to do this if it was what he wanted, and Jim would have developed a customized program just for Sam's company and charged him accordingly.

The debate went back and forth, becoming more and more heated. Complicating the problem was the question of whether Jim should give the remaining four hours of the program and the issue of what was owed. Although Jim remained ready to go on and do the best he could to customize the program, Sam finally told him to forget it. But Jim still wanted to be paid, arguing that he not only had reserved the day for the program but had spent many extra hours preparing it, even if Sam hadn't accurately conveyed what he wanted.

For a time, it looked as if the conflict over Jim's payment was headed for a lawsuit. Sam felt that he didn't owe Jim anything more since Jim hadn't completed the program to Sam's satisfaction. Jim felt that he had completed the program as Sam had explained it and had even done extra work, although it wasn't what Sam now claimed he had expected, so Jim felt he should be paid in full. Besides, Jim argued, he had sent Sam a letter of understanding when Sam had first hired him and Sam had signed it, agreeing to pay.

During the lunch break, Sam considered what to do. He was particularly concerned about having an ugly scene, since Jim fumed he wasn't about to leave unless he got paid as promised the day of the program. But he also didn't want to be browbeaten into paying Jim in full for what he felt was an unsatisfactory program which he had cut off after two hours.

Finally Sam offered a compromise giving Jim about half of the remaining amount due, bringing Jim's payment to about two-thirds of the initial agreed-upon fee. For a moment Jim thought about the alternatives: he would have to sue if he wanted the full amount; even then he might not get everything he wanted; and a lawsuit would take at least several months to pursue. Besides, he would have to invest his energies in trying to put together a suit for a few thousand dollars, as well as trying to collect whatever he won, if anything.

Like Sam, Jim stood to gain by putting the unsuccessful program behind him, rather than trying to fight to maximize what he could gain while risking gaining nothing. And so Jim agreed. Thus, by taking both parties' priorities and interests into account, Sam was able to come up with a good compromise offer that provided a quick resolution for both, which made it easier for Jim to accept.

The Compromising style is useful in the following circumstances:

- When interests are opposed and goals are mutually exclusive, so that a solution depends on each side giving something up

- When you and others don't have time to reach a more comprehensive, far-reaching resolution (as you would in the Collaborating style, for example)

- When you feel that a temporary or short-term resolution, even if it's not ideal, is better than none at all

- When you have tried and failed with other approaches, and a compromise seems to offer the best opportunity for putting the problem behind you and moving on

Compromise Versus Collaboration

Compromise and collaboration have common features—give-and-take, and back-and-forth discussion until a middle ground is reached. The major difference between them is that compromise focuses on surface issues and conflicting wants and needs, which can sometimes be quantified, whereas collaboration involves deeper consideration of the issues and of both parties' positions.

Compromise

Compromise is a common approach to reaching a financial agreement—on a purchase price, a salary amount, a book contract, a real-estate deal, and so on. It can also be especially effective in resolving a conflict over money or value, as in a dispute about the fair price for a product that has not worked as well as expected, or about payment for work that has not been performed to an adequate standard.

In many cases, finding a compromise will entail some back-and-forth bargaining. A good approach is for the parties involved to begin by stating their respective goals—to say what they want and need. Then each party makes offers and counteroffers, usually in turn. It is conventional to begin by somewhat overstating what you want and need, in order to give yourself a better bargaining position, since from that point on you will be giving things up. The key here, however, is not to overstate your wants and needs so much that you are perceived as taking an extreme position. The other party may even feel insulted or consider your offer so out of the ballpark that there is no point discussing your differences at all. If you start off too far from the other party's starting position, the distance between you can interfere with the cooperative spirit that will be needed in order for negotiation to occur in good faith—or at all.

Look for areas of agreement after the initial statement of goals, and then offer your own suggestions for what you might be willing to give up in an exchange, and listen to what the other party would be willing to give up. Then be ready to make additional offers, trade-offs, and bargains, and continue until there is a mutually agreeable arrangement for what will be given up and received in exchange.

It's also possible for one party to come up with a workable solution that strikes a middle ground. If the offer seems fair and reasonable, the other party is likely to agree to it. If you are coming up with a compromise proposal on your own, consider what the other party is likely to value most and what he or she is most likely to give up, and balance these priorities and concerns against your own. Otherwise, your compromise offer will become just another step in the bargaining process, rather than a solution that the other party can readily accept.

Collaboration

In a collaboration, both parties take more time to go beyond their initial positions and examine their own and each other's underlying interests, needs, and concerns. As a result, collaboration typically takes much longer than compromise: there is more discussion and explanation, and each party may need some time to feel comfortable truly expressing his or her views, especially when a difficult situation triggers strong emotions or involves ethical considerations, as well as different views of what constitutes ethical behavior.

Nevertheless, taking time to develop rapport and explore issues is part of the collaborative process. Moreover, the time spent in discussion and exploration can contribute to a resolution that satisfies both parties. That's because this process is designed to allow for full expression of any personal concerns and feelings that may be contributing to the conflict and posing an obstacle to its resolution.

Because collaborating can be more difficult than working out a compromise, and because the situations in which collaboration is used tend to be more complex, it often helps to bring in a neutral third party—a professional mediator, or someone in the organization who is skilled in conflict-resolution techniques and is not involved in the conflict. This person can then facilitate the communication necessary to an effective collaboration, though you and the other party to the conflict can guide the process on your own, if you are both committed to sharing your interests and concerns openly, looking for mutually satisfying alternatives, and taking the necessary time.

Although collaboration does take more time and energy than compromise, it is often the best way to arrive at a comprehensive win-win solution when serious problems are involved Then, achieving this effective long-term resolution will repay the time and energy you spend to fully air and explore the issue.

- When you don't feel that the issue is important enough to warrant a fight for your original goals and objectives, and you would rather pull back and find a more limited but more realistic resolution

- When you feel that giving in a little will benefit your relationship or agreement with others, even if you think you are giving up more than you should

- When you don't have the power to get what you really want, and a compromise will at least give you part of what you hope for

USING THE CONFLICT STYLES

As we have seen, some styles of handling conflict are especially suited to certain types of difficult situations, but your own characteristic style and the styles of others can contribute to the greater effectiveness of one approach over others (refer to Chart 3 for a quick overview). For example, if you are not comfortable acting forcefully in a confrontation, even when you have the power to use the Competing style and good reasons for using it, then it may not be the best one for you: even if it should work, it could leave you feeling upset and stressed about having undermined your relationships with others, and you might be better off with the Collaborating or Compromising style, each of which allows you to achieve your objectives in a more relationship-oriented way. Or, to take another

CHART 3

When to Apply the Five Conflict Styles

Competing

- Issue is important, big stake in outcome
- Have power and authority
- No other options, nothing to lose
- Quick decision needed, emergency situation
- At an impasse, can't get group agreement
- Unpopular decision needed and have power to make it

Avoiding

- Issue is unimportant, little stake in outcome
- Lack power to resolve situation well or at all
- Can't win or low chance of winning
- Need time, want delay to get information or help
- Want to cool down tensions
- Danger of worse conflict if it becomes open
- Others can or will resolve the matter better

Accommodating

- Issue is unimportant, don't care about outcome
- Have little power, no or low chance of winning
- Issue and outcome are more important to others
- Want to keep peace, harmony with others
- Good relationship is more important than issue
- You are wrong, other is right
- Others might learn from situation though wrong

example, say you are involved in a conflict with someone who likes to feel that he is always correct, and who gets upset when he is confronted with information to the contrary or is asked to change what he is doing. He wants to do a good job, but he doesn't take criticism or correction very well. In this case, you know that you are right, and even though you may feel comfortable using the Competing style, you realize that he will probably react defensively to it. Because the

Collaborating

- Issue is important to both
- Similar power or willing to put aside power differences
- Have a close, continuing, interdependent relationship
- Have time and are willing to spend time and effort
- Both able to discuss, listen

Compromising

- Have different goals, and goals not too important
- Have similar power
- Want resolution quickly; temporary resolution okay
- Provides short-term gain
- Fallback when collaboration or competition doesn't work
- Resolution is better than nothing

conflict is over an issue that is not of great importance to you, you decide that it will be best if this person is allowed to recognize for himself that his views are mistaken. Therefore, you choose the Accommodating style as your approach to handling this conflict.

Identifying Conflict Styles

If you are involved in a conflict or difficult situation at work, think about past conflicts in which you have been involved. What has your preferred style of conflict tended to be? What do you know about how the other parties to this conflict have handled past conflicts?

If you and the other parties already have a track record of resolving conflicts together, then your shared history may help you predict how they are likely to react in this case. If there are parties to this conflict with whom you have only recently begun working, then a quick assessment of their personalities may give you some insight into how they are likely to react: Do they seem fairly easygoing and eager to get along? Are they By-the-Bookers?

As for yourself, what conflict style are you most likely to use? To find the answer, you can take the *Thomas–Kilmann Conflict Mode Instrument*. You can also simply review your own responses to past conflicts, think about the conflict style that has been most comfortable for you, and assess how effective your preferred style has been in helping you gain your objectives. If you find that it has not been effective, then you can develop your ability to use other styles. For instance, let's say you tend to use the Accommodating style, and you feel that you get stepped on and taken advantage of as a result. You might practice using the Competing style, as appropriate, perhaps even experimenting with it outside the workplace so that you'll feel more comfortable when the time comes to use it at work. As you pay attention to what you have done in past conflicts and what the results of your behavior have been, you can come to recognize your usual style, determine how well it has worked for you, and decide whether you want to change it.

Rating Your Own Conflict Style

As you review your past handling of conflict, you will probably find that there is one style that you are especially likely to use or prefer. This is your primary style of handling conflict. There may also be one or two styles that you commonly use, but not as often. These are your secondary styles. Or you may have two primary styles, which you use about equally, alternating between them. In this case, you have a bimodal style of handling conflict.

If you have three characteristic styles that you are about equally likely to use, your style of handling conflict would be considered trimodal. Others will have their own styles, too, which will follow the same primary, secondary, bimodal, or trimodal patterns, but it is only through analyzing their behavior in their encounters with you that you will be able to recognize their conflict styles.

You can use Worksheet 12 to help you think about the extent to which you use or prefer to use different styles. Ask yourself which style or styles you use the most, prefer the most, use the least, and feel least comfortable using, and put an "x" in the appropriate box for each style. Then, if you find two or more styles in the same category (for example, you have indicated you use both "Competing" and "Collaborating" the most), rank them, using "1" to indicate your first choice, "2" to indicate your second, and so on. As you make these ratings, write down the first response that comes to mind, since your

WORKSHEET 12

Self-Assessment of Conflict Style

Conflict Style	Use the Most	Prefer Using	Use the Least	Least Like Using
Competing (I actively try to get my own way.)				
Avoiding (I try to avoid conflict.)				
Accommodating (I usually give in to others.)				
Collaborating (I like to take the time to work out a mutually agreeable resolution.)				
Compromising (I typically give up a little in return for getting some of what I want.)				

most spontaneous response is usually the most accurate. The point here is not to think about how you would like to respond in the current conflict, or in the future; just think about how you have responded to situations of conflict in general, and know that a thorough assessment of your past behavior is the first step in changing your conflict style if you decide that a change is in order.

CHAPTER 7

Using Negotiation
Effectively

If you have chosen a conflict style that involves competition, avoidance, or accommodation, then you are probably not going to be using negotiation—unless you are using these conflict styles in the context of a more elaborate negotiation process, for the purpose of improving your bargaining position. In general, however, negotiation comes into play when you try to resolve a difficult situation through compromise or collaboration.

SEEKING A WIN-WIN SOLUTION

When you negotiate, it is unnecessary to imagine that you are in a win-lose battle in which victory must be gained at all costs and the other side defeated. This is particularly true in the workplace, where you and the other parties are likely to continue working together, coming into contact, or moving along adjacent paths, and where the comments and opinions of others can shape your future career opportunities. In these circumstances, the long term is an important consideration, even though you may come out ahead, for the moment, in a compromise or collaboration: short-term gains that leave unhappy losers in their wake can come back to hurt you.

Therefore, whether you seek to compromise or collaborate, it is best to think in terms of working toward a win-win solution.

A win-win solution leaves all parties feeling some sense of satisfaction in what they have gained, even if it isn't all they wanted. The way to work toward a win-win solution is to look for underlying reasons, interests, and needs, identify priorities for yourself and the other parties, and then use either or both of the following two strategies:

1. Give concessions, and seek to get the other parties to do the same, in order to obtain offers that satisfy your highest priorities.

2. Seek new alternatives that offer satisfactory payoffs for you and the other parties.

There is often more than one reason for a conflict, even if the parties on both sides think it has broken out for one particular reason. Therefore, identifying all the possible reasons for the conflict is the key to resolving it in a way that offers enough mutual benefit that all the parties find it more in their interest to resolve the conflict than to let it continue.

STEPS IN A SUCCESSFUL NEGOTIATION

The steps in a successful negotiation are similar to the elements of the ERI model. These steps are described in the following sections.

Get Emotions Under Control

In general, people involved in a conflict have deeply held negative feelings, even if they don't express them. When these feelings do not arise from the underlying factors that have led to the conflict, they are produced by it.

Before you can negotiate effectively or deal successfully with the conflict in any other way, all the people involved in it have to get their emotions under control. Then it will be possible to move on to a reasonable examination of underlying interests, concerns, and needs. (You may want to revisit Chapter 2 for tips on controlling and working with strong emotions.) Whatever you do, remember that the goal at this point is to release your own emotions and help the other parties release theirs, so that you can coolly and calmly address the issue together and work toward its resolution. Therefore, don't get trapped into exploring and processing these feelings, and all the possible reasons for them, at any great length. Although some people find this kind of analysis therapeutic, it generally perpetuates the problem.

Set Ground Rules

Once emotions have been brought under control, it is time to set the ground rules for the negotiation process. Sometimes it will be enough to mention the ground rules briefly, as when you are trying to work things out with someone who is experienced in resolving conflicts, or when the other party seems impatient or in a hurry. At other times it may be a good idea to review the ground rules in greater detail, as when the other party is unfamiliar with this more reasoned approach to conflict resolution; this is what professional mediators and community conciliators usually do when they begin a conflict-resolution process.

Either way, take the initiative, if you can, in discussing the ground rules, and explain, as necessary, that they are intended to help the negotiation process go smoothly. Among other basic rules to suggest or discuss, the parties to the negotiation can agree to do the following:

- Listen to each other as carefully as possible

- Refrain from interrupting each other

- Refrain from expressing anger or hostility, even if there is strong disagreement

- Treat each other with respect

- Spend an agreed-upon amount of time on the negotiation process

- Try to see each other's points of view

Whether the ground rules are explicitly stated or implicitly agreed to, they work because they establish a tone of mutual respect and fair play, and so they help prepare the way for a productive negotiation. (In general, when ground rules are suggested by a mediator or community conciliator at a conflict-resolution session, the parties agree

Understanding Another Person's Position and Concerns

I first offered these guidelines in my book *Resolving Conflict With Others and Within Yourself* and include them again here in the context of resolving difficult situations in the workplace.

Look at the World Through the Other Person's Eyes

If you can imagine what another person is thinking or perceiving, you are better able to assess what he or she feels is important and what he or she might be most willing to give up. You don't have to agree with the other person's point of view. If you understand it, however, you will have more empathy and greater rapport, and it will be easier for you to negotiate and use persuasion in reaching a more favorable agreement: when you appear to understand another person's point of view, he or she is apt to trust you more.

Avoid Judgments

Withhold judgment about what the other person thinks, believes, or has done. You probably think your own point of view is correct, and the other person may feel the same way about his or her own viewpoint. Even if you are certain that the other person is clearly wrong, however, that may not be an easy admission for him or her to make. Moreover, in many situations there is no absolute right or wrong; there are just different opinions and perspectives. Therefore, even if it's your usual style to be judgmental, it is best not to criticize or blame the other person, even when he or she has made a mistake or holds incorrect assumptions or beliefs. If you do, the other person is likely to become defensive and more resistant to your own ideas, and he or she could even attack you in order to level the playing field and feel better. Once a negative exchange of this kind has begun, negotiation easily breaks down as anger escalates, and the original conflict becomes more difficult to resolve because there is now an additional layer of anger and hurt feelings. If the other person judges, criticizes, or blames you, the best strategy is to remain cool and not respond with defensiveness. Instead, use the "water off a duck's back" response: just let the negative judgments roll off, and refocus the discussion on the negotiation process. Keep your goal of resolution in sight. Don't get caught up in side issues. Stay with your original agenda, and move ahead.

Discuss Differences

To a greater or lesser extent, your perceptions, assumptions, and beliefs are different from the other person's. If you can discuss these differences, you can more easily avoid the misunderstandings that often become a major stumbling block in negotiations. This is the time to correct any misinformation about you that the other person may have received. If you do offer such a correction, do it respectfully, so that the other person won't feel put down for being wrong; simply suggest that each of you may have formed a different understanding of your behavior, and say that you hope to clear up any misperceptions or confusion. As necessary, provide supporting evidence for your point of view, such as documents or statements from a third party. When you use this kind of neutral, fact-based approach to correcting the record, the other person may find that it's more acceptable to change his or her point of view.

Keep the Other Person Involved

Even if you decide to take the lead in the negotiation process, involve the other person. That way, he or she will be more inclined to have an investment in the process, feel that he or she has contributed good ideas, and recognize his or her stake in the outcome. If the other person comes to feel that you are trying to impose your own agenda, he or she may offer only resistance or even outright rejection of your proposals. There are several ways for you to keep the other person involved:

1. Encourage the other person to contribute suggestions for solving the problem.

2. If you can, present your ideas in such a way that they are linked to something the other person has said, or to what you think the other person believes or perceives. For example, if you

think that he or she tends to like concrete facts and details, offer facts and give details to back them up. If you think that he or she is more of an idea person and most interested in the big picture, describe your ideas in terms of a larger context and say what they mean to him or her personally and to the organization in general.

3. If what the other person proposes is what you want or something you have already said, accept and support this proposal as if it were actually his or her own idea (unless, of course, he or she points out that it originated with you). Don't come back with a remark like "I already said that." It sounds too much like "I told you so," which can only make the other person feel put down, defensive, and inclined to back away from what you want. If you let the other person believe that the proposal is his or her own, he or she will feel more ownership of the idea and will be more willing to adopt it, thereby supporting your own point of view.

Be Reasonable and Realistic

If you are reasonable and realistic when you first state your goals and needs, you will be more likely to further a good-faith, cooperative negotiation. The process will be imbued with a spirit of fairness, and the other person will be encouraged to feel more trust in the process—and in you. Reasonable and realistic initial goals foster a win-win solution, whereas unrealistic ones weighted too much in your favor foster an adversarial proceeding in which a win for you is a loss for the other. If you state reasonable goals and the other person becomes more assertive and forceful, seeking to take advantage of your desire to be fair, a good strategy is to remain firm and emphasize your desire to find a mutually agreeable, fair solution. If the other person really does want to work out a resolution, he or she generally will see that being too forceful won't work, whereas seeking resolution through compromise or collaboration might. Moreover, many people have an internal sense of justice, and this is another reason why an appeal for fairness may be effective.

as a matter of course; if they are unable to agree on ground rules, it's usually a sign that the particular issue cannot be negotiated, and that a different resolution process will be needed.) Therefore, propose any ground rules that you feel are appropriate; just be sure that the other party agrees and willingly states or acknowledges this agreement.

Once ground rules have been established, they can be referred to if the negotiation breaks down or if anger suddenly erupts. If such a breakdown should occur, it's a signal to stop for a while, bring any negative feelings back under control, and then (and only then) get the negotiation process back on track. If not, you will need to find another approach.

Clarify Issues and Positions

With emotions under control and ground rules in place, it's time for both sides to clarify the issues and their respective positions, interests, and points of view. To the extent possible, find out first what the other party or parties' points of view are, and what they want and need. This knowledge will help you take the views and concerns of the other party or parties into consideration as you shape your own proposals. You still hope to gain your own objectives as best you can, of course. Nevertheless, by letting the other party or parties know that you want to listen, and by urging them to put their concerns on the table first, you not only help them feel heard and understood but also improve your chances of shaping the process and getting a positive reception for your own views.

Explore Needs, Interests, and Concerns

To take this step, both sides share information about what they really want and need. The parties go beyond their initial positions to examine why they have taken these positions. You can use the following methods to seek this kind of information:

1. *Ask why the other party has taken his or her particular position.* That way, you will gain a better understanding of what the other party really needs, wants, expects, hopes for, is afraid of, or otherwise finds important enough to justify his or her position. If you know what is really going on, you are in a better position to

change the other party's attitude toward your own goals by coming up with alternatives that may appeal to both of you. For example, if you know why a particular company policy exists, you may be able to replace it with a less restrictive alternative that still satisfies the underlying concern. For instance, say you want to work at home on a project, but the company policy requires everyone to be in the office at certain times. Once you start asking questions and examining the rationale for this policy, you discover that the boss is afraid employees will be less productive if they don't have supervision, and that he wants people available for meetings. You can then propose an alternative way in which you can meet his two objections while working at home, such as by filing regular progress reports and using a pager. But be careful here: when you ask questions and seek changes, do so in a tactful, diplomatic way, so that the other party is not left feeling defensive but instead becomes more amenable to accommodating your suggestions.

2. *Ask why the other party has not accepted your own position.* This question needs to be handled a bit more sensitively, but if you ask in a way that is neutral and implies no accusation, the other party's answer may give you helpful information that you can use in the future, perhaps to make your own position more appealing next time. "Why didn't you . . . ?" is confrontational; the other party is essentially being asked to defend his or her actions. "What were your reasons for choosing not to . . . ? I'd really like to understand" is a neutral request for information. Listen carefully to the explanations; they may point to obstacles and suggest future strategies for achieving your goals.

3. *As you ask questions, listen for multiple interests.* Because there is generally more than one explanation for why a person holds a particular position, try to find out what all the other party's rationales are, and give yours as well. That way, you will both gain insight into complementary concerns or areas of mutual agreement and will be better able to determine appropriate trade-offs. Make an assessment of your relative priorities at the same time, to help you in proposing trade-offs. Of course, as the number of

parties to a negotiation increases, so does the number of rationales and priorities. To prevent confusion, you may want to make
a list of the rationales that the other parties give and of who
wants want. (You can do this as concerns are being shared, or you
can do it later.) Keep track of your own and others' rationales
and priorities; for example, circle the most important ones on the
list, and underline those that are secondary but still of high
importance. As the negotiation continues, this list can help you
decide what to offer and what to request in return.

4. *Talk about your own interests and needs.* Just as hearing what others
   want and need helps you weigh what to offer and what to
   expect, others will find it helpful to hear information about your
   own interests and needs. Moreover, as you share information
   about your limits, others can better understand and empathize
   with your problems and may lower their expectations accordingly. For example, if you are involved in a dispute with an
   employee over salary or benefits, mention your budgetary
   constraints and the way your own supervisor is monitoring
   your department at the same time that you compliment the
   employee on his or her valuable contributions to your department. Then, to compensate for the budgetary constraints, you
   may find other areas for negotiation (such as giving extra time
   off or making scheduling changes).

5. *When you discuss your own interests, also demonstrate empathy and
   fairness.* Show that you recognize and understand the other
   party's needs and concerns, and that you don't want to minimize
   their importance. It can also be helpful to state your rationales,
   interests, and needs before you state your position. Doing so
   helps provide a meaningful context, so that the other party is
   more able to understand why you feel as you do or have the limitations and restrictions that you have; he or she can then be
   more receptive to what you are saying. For example, the boss
   who has to announce reassignments due to budget cuts might do
   best to make this announcement only after she has praised her
   employees for their work, described how difficult things have
   been, and explained that, now more than ever, she needs their

cooperation. The news isn't good, no matter how the boss frames it, but this approach cushions the blow and elicits less anger and resentment than the simple edict that certain employees are being transferred, with little or no explanation. This kind of forthright explanation also prepares the way for more comfortable negotiations about the details of the reassignments.

Explore the Alternatives

Once you know each other's wants and needs, you are now ready to generate and discuss alternative resolutions that meet the requirements and desires of parties on both sides of the negotiation. For more information about exploring alternatives, especially through the use of brainstorming techniques, see Chapter 8; for now, keep the following principles in mind:

1. *Be spontaneous, and come up with as many possibilities as you can.* Don't try to evaluate or critique your ideas while you are generating them. Suspend judgment for now. You can use your reason later on to choose the best alternatives.

2. *Keep your focus on the future.* Even after you and others have released negative emotions and discussed your rationales and needs, you may be tempted to revisit some feelings or offer additional explanations and justifications. It's generally best not to do either unless you feel that the negotiation process was so rushed that feelings were left unexpressed and concerns were left hanging, so that a sense of wariness and mistrust is getting in the way. If you must, you can go back and work through earlier steps in the negotiation process, but do try hard to resist the urge, and if someone else brings up feelings or explanations, gently interrupt. Acknowledge the feelings, and say that you can understand them, but express your hope that you can now focus on resolving the problem rather than dwelling on the factors that may have created it.

3. *Remain open to others' ideas and alternatives.* Although it's a good idea to begin a negotiation with your own agenda and a clear idea of what you hope to gain, be receptive to others' ideas, and

be ready to modify your own. There are many viable possibilities for resolving any conflict, so consider all of them. That way, you won't squelch new ideas yourself or prematurely cut other parties off from the possibility of introducing them. You will also be more open to making an honest evaluation of new ideas and, as a result, more likely to get a better and more widely accepted resolution.

4. *Don't be too quick to settle on a single alternative.* The appropriate amount of time to spend on exploring alternatives will differ for different groups and in different situations. The key is to find the balance point at which the idea-generation process slows down and the parties to the negotiation feel satisfied that they have sufficiently explored the various options. Naturally, you won't want to spend time and energy trying to think of still more ideas after the initial creative phase of idea production. But you also won't want to embrace a resolution too quickly or prematurely settle for the first one that seems plausible and acceptable. The tendency to jump at an early resolution can be a strong one, since we all have a desire for closure. This kind of quick acceptance can be fine if all the parties feel truly comfortable with a particular resolution. If you sense any doubts, however, or if you feel that the resolution may have been reached too quickly for people to have fully accepted it, ask whether everyone truly is comfortable with it. If not, continue exploring. True, it will now take more time and energy to reach a resolution, but an issue that is important enough will warrant making that extra investment.

Reach Agreement on the Best Win-Win Option

As you propose the solutions that you prefer, explain or frame them in a way that shows the other party how he or she will benefit. That way, you emphasize the win-win properties of your proposed solutions, and you encourage the other party to respond in kind. At the same time, this approach helps you recognize which options offer the strongest possibilities for a win-win resolution.

To guide the process toward closure, help the other party feel comfortable making concessions. Doing this will be especially important if you encounter resistance as the other party moves from his or her initial position and feels a sense of loss at giving up certain interests and abandoning particular concerns. Be reassuring, and try to help the other party feel more comfortable about finding a resolution that is mutually agreeable. For example, point out what both of you are gaining in exchange for the concessions. Remember, too, that some people find the act of giving up or giving in particularly hard—they see it as a personal defeat—so help the other party save face and maintain a sense of self-esteem. Praise the other party for any concessions, point out that you understand the difficulties involved in negotiating this issue, and show how much you appreciate his or her contribution to the negotiation process.

You may also offer an additional concession of your own; even a minor one can help ease the other party's sense of loss or defeat and contribute to a collaborative spirit, which will make the remaining details of the negotiation go more smoothly and support the success of the negotiated resolution. And if you have nothing more that you can concede, just express your appreciation for the other party's contributions to the process of finding a solution.

WORKING WITH INTUITION

The two chapters in Part 3 highlight three key techniques for tapping and using the intuitive faculty, as the third step in using the ERI model. Chapter 8 discusses brainstorming, a technique that can be used to develop alternatives. Chapter 9 offers a guide to visualization (used in developing ideas and imagining possibilities) and self-talk (used in developing ideas and making choices). These techniques have a variety of applications, ranging from generating new concepts and improving project management to promoting personal development and more harmonious relationships. In these two chapters, we will focus specifically on their uses in resolving workplace conflicts and other difficult issues. With their help, you can develop and strengthen your sense of knowing the best approach to any difficult situation.

CHAPTER 8

Brainstorming

After you have recognized that there is a problem—whether you're confronting a conflict, a difficult person, or another issue—a key step is to generate and weigh different possibilities for solving that problem. One way to do this is to use the technique of brainstorming.

Brainstorming is typically viewed as a facilitator-guided activity performed in groups of various sizes—perhaps as few as two or three people to as many as two dozen. However, brainstorming in groups is only one example of how this technique can be used. This group approach favors the kind of thinker who is able to come up with ideas quickly, and who can be uninhibited about sharing them on the spot. You can also use brainstorming by yourself to generate new ideas in a more personal, more reflective way. The basics of brainstorming will be familiar to most readers, but we'll review them briefly on the following pages.

In phase 1, you tap your intuition in order to come up with as many solutions as you can. You don't attempt to evaluate, critique, or choose among the ideas being offered; you just stay in this creative and receptive mode for as long as you have new ideas, letting them flow without time constraints or controls on what you experience.

It's very important to come to the brainstorming process with an open mind, especially if the problem involves many diverse parties,

When (and When Not) to Brainstorm

Brainstorming can be used to find resolutions for a variety of workplace conflicts, whether they involve individual or group issues. For example, you can use brainstorming in any of the following situations:

- When you are experiencing a personality conflict with a manager, an employee, or a co-worker and are not sure what the most effective approach would be

- When you need to reorganize your work group for higher productivity and want to determine the best reorganization plan

- When there is a conflict between your company and the larger community over the company's expansion plans, and you want to figure out the best resolution

Whatever the problem, brainstorming can shake you out of old habits so that you can consider the greatest number of alternatives and choose the best one for your situation.

In general, individual brainstorming is well suited to interpersonal issues in the workplace (for example, the problem of relating to a difficult person), whereas group brainstorming is especially suited to group- and organization-level issues. In some cases, however, individual brainstorming can help in solving a group-level problem, as when a manager or other company official uses individual brainstorming to reach a decision about how best to approach a problem involving a work team or an issue that affects the company as a whole. Conversely, sometimes an individual may bring a personal conflict (such as a dispute with a co-worker) to a small group of people (an outside support group, for example, or a close-knit work team) who are not involved with the situation. (In this case, of course, it's a good idea to conceal the identity of any involved parties who are not present.) In yet another scenario, both parties to a personal dispute may bring their conflict to a group and seek the opinions and guidance of others in solving the problem.

As useful as brainstorming is, however, there are times when it is better not to use this technique—or, if you do use it, to set clear limits on its use:

- Don't use brainstorming to come up with alternatives that will not be viable. Perhaps company policies or other factors are constraining the possibilities; whatever the situation, explain the constraints before the brainstorming session begins. That way, the process won't generate unworkable options and leave the participants feeling discouraged and ineffective. In a situation of this kind, keep the brainstorming process focused solely on problems and issues where the alternatives being considered can actually have an effect.

- Don't use brainstorming in a group where there are serious personality conflicts and difficulties with teamwork. If brainstorming is used in this situation, some individuals may feel inhibited about sharing their ideas, and others may use the process to show off or put other participants down. A better approach is to use individual brainstorming as a way of finding ideas for solving the group's problems.

multiple causes, and multiple possible outcomes. Therefore, in phase 1, keep your conscious, rational, critical mind—your internal "judge"—out of the way. If you need help silencing your judging faculty during this phase, try the following exercise (this is an example of visualization, a technique described more thoroughly in Chapter 9):

Take a few moments to get relaxed. Now, in your mind's eye, see yourself picking up all your old ideas or habits that haven't worked. See yourself putting them into a box and sealing it with tape. Now see yourself putting this box high up on a closet shelf. Push the box all the way to the back of the shelf, cover it with a blanket, and close the closet door. Now turn and walk away. As you leave the box behind in the closet, know that your old ideas and habits are now in the past. You are free to take them out again and use them whenever you choose, but you are also free to put them away for as long as you want to.

In phase 2, you begin to let your internal judge assess and evaluate the new ideas, set priorities among them, and make choices. You now attempt to arrive at a decision about the most suitable alternative or alternatives for solving the problem, using reasoned analysis and calling on your inner knowledge or wisdom—your intuition.

BRAINSTORMING ON YOUR OWN

Focus on the problem, and, as quickly as possible, think of as many ways to resolve it as you can. The most common method is to make a written list of the ideas that come to you. If you feel more comfortable saying your ideas aloud as they come to you, recite them into a tape recorder and then play the tape back and write the ideas down as you listen.

It is usually helpful to frame the issue in the following way: "What should I do about . . . ?" State the problem very specifically. Avoid vague questions like "How can I resolve the trouble in my work group?" Instead, focus on the exact difficulty: "How can I deal with the way some members' lack of enthusiasm has been interfering with the group's morale over the past few weeks?"

If you have a very broad question, or one that concerns a complicated problem, divide the question up into several specific parts and then brainstorm ideas for each one. For example, if you are thinking about a change of career, a question like "What kind of position do I want to find in a new field?" could be divided up into "What kind of field do I want to get into?" and "What type of company in this field do I want to work for?" and "What type of work do I want to do in this company?" It can sometimes be helpful to imagine that an expert teacher or guide is assisting you with this problem or that you are giving someone else advice about the problem. In the first case, you gain help from a mentor; in the second case, you give yourself some distance from the problem that can help you be more detached and objective as you brainstorm ideas.

Phase 1: Generating and Recording Ideas

Whether you initially write or tape your ideas, and whether you are at home or at work, do it in a quiet, private place where you will be free from distractions. Write or speak quickly so as not to lose your train of thought, and don't think yet about whether the ideas are valuable. Just let them come, and write them down.

When the problem or situation is a simple one, you may need only ten or fifteen minutes to come up with many viable alternatives and choose among them. When the problem or situation is more complex, allow more time—perhaps twenty to thirty minutes or longer. As you gain experience with the brainstorming process, you will probably need less time, since you will be more in touch with your intuition and better at coming up with ideas.

You will find that one idea triggers another: as you let your ideas flow, their momentum triggers your writing or speaking and recording process, which in turn helps you generate more ideas by triggering your creativity. The more you use this free-flowing process, the freer your mind becomes.

If the ideas don't come at first (as can happen if you're new at brainstorming), continue to focus on the problem for the allotted time. Focusing your attention will help get the ideas started, and one idea will start the flow of more. Then, whenever any idea pops into your mind, or even the wispy fragment of an idea, write it down, or say it aloud into your tape recorder. If you find that you're slowing down, stop when the allotted time is up. If the ideas are still flowing freely, however, keep going. When the flow eventually tapers off, allow a final minute or two for any last thoughts, and perhaps prod yourself with the question: "Can I think of any more ideas that can help me with this situation?" Then, in this receptive frame of mind, wait and see if any more ideas come. When you feel that the flow of ideas has come to an end and the process is complete, stop.

Phase 2: Evaluating Ideas

After you have finished generating ideas, go over them and rate them on a scale of 0 (not very good) to 5 (the best). Photocopy Worksheet 13 and use it to help you rate the alternatives that your brainstorming session has produced. If you think an idea needs further development—for example, if you discover that you will need to plan a series of steps for implementing a particular idea—go through the brainstorming process once again, focusing on what still has to be done. You are now ready to put your highest-rated ideas into practice to solve the problem.

WORKSHEET 13

Brainstorming Ideas and Alternatives

The problem or issue I want to brainstorm:

_____

_____

_____

Possible Solutions	How I Rate These Ideas (0-5)
1.	
2.	
3.	
4.	
5.	
6.	
7.	
8.	
9.	
10.	
11.	
12.	
13.	
14.	

BRAINSTORMING IN A GROUP

If you are going to be brainstorming with others—the ideal approach when the problem concerns a team or a group, or when you want outside input on an individual problem—find a place (such as a conference room) where everyone can focus on the issue without distraction. Everyone should agree to participate and stay focused on the issue about which you want to brainstorm.

If you have brought your own problem to a group that is not involved in it, state the problem for the group members, using the guidelines given earlier. Then let them do the brainstorming, perhaps with a facilitator, while you remain silent, listen, and write their ideas down. In some cases, if you feel inspired to join in, it may be fine for you to add your own ideas to those of the group. If you inject yourself too actively or too aggressively into the brainstorming process, however, you will cut it short—and, after all, you are here to listen to the group members' ideas.

As you listen, avoid "Yes, but . . . " responses if you hear ideas that you have already considered and rejected, or if you think of reasons why an idea won't work. This type of critical reaction will tend to make others feel defensive and uncomfortable about sharing. Just let others freely offer ideas while you refrain from commenting.

If you are using a group to brainstorm a problem in which the group is involved, one group member should be chosen to facilitate the process. If you are able to adopt a neutral stance that encourages others to participate, you can take the facilitator role yourself, especially if you are experienced in this role. But if your taking this role would make it difficult for others to participate freely—say, if you are the boss and are asking employees for their input, or if you are a lower-status employee and higher-status group members might feel uncomfortable or inhibited with you in this leadership role—you should ask someone else to be the facilitator. According to the circumstances, this person might be a group member who is also a skilled facilitator, or you might bring in a neutral outsider who is experienced in leading groups.

Phase 1: Generating and Recording Ideas

To begin the process, choose a group recorder to write down ideas as they are generated. This person should use a large sheet of paper or flip chart visible to everyone. It is best if the recorder is someone other than the person facilitating the group, so that recording won't interfere with the facilitation process. (If the group is large enough, it may help to have two recorders writing in turn on different sheets so that no information evaporates if ideas come fast and furiously.) The recorder should not write down the names or initials of people suggesting ideas; it takes extra time, makes the process more formal, may introduce an element of competition, and may make participants self-conscious and therefore less willing to say what they think.

It is a good idea for everyone to sit in a circle. This seating arrangement reinforces the sense that all contributions will have equal value. The face-to-face contact is also more informal and encourages spontaneity.

It also helps to establish a rough timeline for brainstorming—about ten to fifteen minutes for a simple problem, and fifteen to thirty minutes if it's more complex. If the flow of ideas tapers off before the time is up, the time limit can be reduced; if the group has an abundance of ideas, the time limit can be extended.

If the members of the group haven't brainstormed together before, provide a brief introduction to the process. Make it shorter if the participants are familiar with brainstorming but have not done it together before. Point out that participants can expand on ideas that have been offered but should not analyze or evaluate them; remind the group that ideas will be recorded for later evaluation.

With these preliminaries out of the way, pose a clear, specific question and invite everyone to begin brainstorming. If the idea-generation phase seems to have reached an end, it's still important to ask if there are any final ideas; you may get a few more good ones that way.

Phase 2: Evaluating Ideas

Evaluation is generally conducted with the whole group. When the group is very large, however, an alternative is to have a smaller subgroup do an initial culling of the suggestions, either selecting the best ideas or putting similar ideas into clusters for the whole group to evaluate.

As in the process of individual brainstorming, the group can rate the brainstormed suggestions on a scale of 0 to 5; see Worksheet 11. These ratings should be made quickly and intuitively, without interference from the rational, critical mind. If you think an idea has possibilities but are not sure, of if you feel that it needs more development through additional brainstorming, place a question mark for that idea in the rating column.

If all the group members are going to rate the suggestions to-gether, it is a good idea to have the recorder read each suggestion aloud. The group members then vote, with a show of hands, on how they want to score each idea—as a 5, a 4, a 3, and so on. The recorder adds up the total score for each idea, divides that total by the number of people who have voted, and produces an average score for each idea. Another method, which can be used if there are a great many ideas, is to ask each person to select between three and five of his or her personal favorites (those ideas that he or she has rated with a score of 5) and, of that group, vote only for those ideas that he or she likes the most. With this method, you keep the ideas that have gotten the most votes, and you eliminate the others. You can then use weighted voting or another kind of elimination process until you come up with the best of these top ideas. Use the review and selec-tion process that works best for your group, and plan to spend about ten to twenty minutes on this process—longer if people are being really creative.

Finally, revisit the top-rated ideas (those that have been rated with a score of 5). In general, these will be the ones to develop and imple-ment first. If there are still too many ideas in the top-rated group, rate this group again, and from this second list take the top-rated ideas—those that have been rated with a score of 5 in both rounds, or with a score of 5 in the first round and 4 in the other. (You can leave the lower-rated scores for later.) You now return to brainstorming, to decide how best to implement the top ideas (for example, if the key to solving the problem is to reorganize the office, brainstorm about how to do that).

MOVING FROM IDEAS TO ACTION

A good way to put your ideas into action is to create and share a timeline showing the date (as early as possible) by which the measures needed to solve the problem will be taken. For example, put an announcement in the office newsletter, or post your plans on the office bulletin board. Then, as you make the necessary changes, keep everyone informed about your progress. You can use Worksheet 12, on the following page, to set up your own action plan. The dates can be changed, as necessary; what's important is that you have a map for the journey toward resolution.

WORKSHEET 14

Plan of Action for Resolving a Difficult Situation

Steps to Resolution	Date to Begin	Date to Complete
1.		
2.		
3.		
4.		
5.		
6.		
7.		
8.		
9.		
10.		
11.		
12.		
13.		
14.		
15.		
16.		
17.		
18.		
19.		
20.		

Brainstorming Resolves Problems
in a Companywide Project

Paul's company wanted to host some community events for public relations purposes. Initially the CEO had asked eight division heads to work together on the project. However, she had left the guidelines vague as to what kinds of events should be planned and who was to do what. As a result, the division heads began to work independently on making contacts in the community to promote events they personally favored. Support from within the company was no less divided, with some responding enthusiastically, some offering support in return for participation in their pet projects, and others expressing no interest at all. The process of setting up a companywide community program had resulted in political infighting within the company rather than a united public relations effort.

Paul was given the job of sorting out the mess. He was ideally suited to the task since he was not involved in implementing any of the ideas and he was adept at group facilitation. He invited the eight division leaders to come together for a group planning meeting to organize a joint project that everyone could support. The meeting was held in a large conference room with a round table, and Paul stood apart from the group with a flip chart and magic markers, so he could record what people said.

Paul set the stage by acknowledging that there had been problems in organizing a program in the past and stressing that the key to making this project work was putting aside past differences and focusing on the future. Rather than seeing this meeting as a forum to gain support for the projects they had previously suggested, the division managers should consider a range of ideas—those they had promoted in the past, those others had suggested, and any they might come up with today. Then the group as a whole could select the ideas it wanted to work on and figure out how to join forces behind them. He emphasized that past ideas and new ideas would be considered equally—so this was the perfect opportunity to brainstorm possibilities.

Next, after explaining the basic ground rules of brainstorming and explaining that he would be writing down every idea anyone suggested, Paul began the process. Though the division managers started by suggesting their original ideas, Paul encouraged them to think of additional possibilities, and soon they were tossing out more and more ideas. In fact, it turned into a kind of competitive game for them to see how many ideas they could come up with.

After Paul had about two dozen ideas listed, he asked the division managers to vote on their favorites. Aware of the way the process had previously led to conflict and the formation of political alliances, rather than inviting the managers to vote openly, he asked them to vote on slips of paper. Also, to discourage the managers from voting for only their own pet projects, he asked them to vote for their five favorites and rank them from 1 to 5. After gathering the votes, Paul tallied the numbers and came up with scores for the projects. He asked the managers to vote again on the three projects that had received the most votes and rate them from 1 to 3. This time, he was able to announce the clear winner—a program to mentor at-risk high school students and direct them away from crime, violence, and truancy and toward learning about business and work opportunities and how to succeed in life.

As a result of this brainstorming process, each of the division managers felt that he or she had had a hand in deciding on the program, so they could all enthusiastically support it. Using similar brainstorming techniques, Paul next led the group in deciding what steps it might take to initiate the program and what roles members of the company might play in implementing it. Finally, once these action steps and roles had been developed, it was an easy process to assign the tasks to the division managers, who now felt they were part of a team spearheading the project and were ready to bring in their own employees to participate in the program under their leadership.

CHAPTER 9

Using Visualization
and Self-Talk

Brainstorming, as we saw in Chapter 8, can be very helpful in coming up with options, especially when a problem is very difficult or complex. In this chapter, we will examine visualization and self-talk, tools for intuitively sharpening your focus on your chosen options and exploring how you feel about these choices. As you use these intuitive tools for resolving difficult situations in the workplace, you will find that they have other uses as well—for example, helping you set goals, manage projects, and increase your efficiency and productivity. Day-to-day practice with these techniques will make their use easy and nearly automatic, so that you'll often be able to see possibilities and make spontaneous choices in a matter of seconds.

VISUALIZATION

Visualization, or mental imaging (the terms are basically synonymous), involves seeing possible alternatives and solutions in your mind's eye. To use this technique, you need to be in a receptive state of mind.

There are many ways to visualize in developing ideas for resolving conflicts, or for other purposes. Here, we will focus on one very effective way of visualizing: consulting your Inner Expert. You can visualize in this way by yourself or in a group.

USING YOUR INNER EXPERT

Your Inner Expert can give you advice in any kind of situation and can assume a variety of personae—a teacher, for example, or a guide or guru. For individuals with strong spiritual or religious interests, the Inner Expert may take the form of a spiritual helper, an angel, an animal guardian, or some other kind of counselor. Someone with a more technological bent might have an Inner Expert who is an all-knowing computer or robot or perhaps call on an imagined scientist or professor. You can visualize or conceptualize your Inner Expert in whatever form you prefer, since you are basically giving symbolic form to your unconscious voice or inner seeing, in order to get in touch with it, communicate with it, and gain insights from it. In other words, you transform an unconscious, knowledgeable part of yourself into a form with which you can have direct, conscious, informative communication.

As in brainstorming, when you call on your Inner Expert you are drawing on your intuitive, creative abilities to solve a problem or resolve a conflict drawing on your "right brain" holistic way of seeing. In contrast with brainstorming, however, you don't try to come up with as many quick ideas as you would from an alert, active, state of mind. Instead, you enter into a very relaxed and almost trancelike state, akin to mild hypnosis or deep meditation, where you focus your attention within a very receptive way.

Once you have entered this state, you make contact with your Inner Expert. You see your Inner Expert's face on a TV screen or a computer monitor, or you hear your Inner Expert's voice giving advice over a radio, or you have a conversation with your Inner Expert in the setting of a workshop or a classroom, or you perceive your Inner Expert as a present-day or historical figure or as someone you already know (a parent, a close relative, a good friend).

You pose your questions, and the answers come as intuitive flashes of insight, telling you the next steps to take in working with a problem.

As you first learn to make contact with your Inner Expert, you can use the following exercise to help you with relaxation and visualization. (Later on, after you have gained some experience with this technique, you probably won't need to go through this entire exercise; instead, you'll be able to contact your Inner Expert almost automatically by getting into a relaxed state and asking him or her to appear.) You can read this exercise to yourself before you go through it, or tape it and then relax and visualize while you play the tape back; you can also ask someone else to read the exercise to you. When advice comes from your Inner Expert, you can write it down as you hear it, if writing won't distract you. In general, however, it's best to wait until right after you have finished the exercise, when the advice you have gained is still fresh in your mind; if you try to write the information down while receiving it, the left-brain activity of writing could pull you out of your receptive, right-brain state and reduce the amount of information you receive. Another possibility is to speak into a tape recorder as you receive advice.

To begin this exercise, close your eyes and take several deep breaths. When you feel very comfortable and relaxed, think of the difficult situation that you want to resolve. In your mind's eye, see the problem occurring right now. Even if you are part of the situation, imagine that you are looking at it now as an outsider. As you watch, ask a question about what to do. Make your question as specific as you can.

With your question in mind, return your focus to your breathing. Breathe deeply in, and then breathe out, in and out, very calm and relaxed. Feel yourself getting very comfortable as you observe your breath going in and out, in and out. Yet even as you become very relaxed, you are still able to stay alert and awake and listen to these directions.

Now, in your mind's eye, see yourself in a special place where you feel very comfortable and very safe. It may be your room. It may be your private office. It may be a meadow or a lake or a place in the country where you like to go to relax. You see yourself there now, and you begin to notice what's around you. If you're indoors, maybe you see books and a computer screen. If you're outdoors, maybe you see trees and grass. You feel very, very comfortable.

Now you see someone coming toward you. This person is someone who can help you with the information and advice that you need. Maybe you have seen this person before, or maybe this is your first meeting. Maybe you know this person because he or she has helped you before. Or maybe this person is someone completely new to you. Just say hello, and know that this person is your Inner Expert and has come here to help you and give you information.

Invite your Inner Expert to sit down with you. Now spend a little time getting to know this person, or getting to know him or her better. Ask who he or she is, what he or she does, and what he or she is especially knowledgeable about.

Listen to the answer. Now tell your Inner Expert something about yourself and the situation you want to resolve. As you describe your situation, you see that this person is very sympathetic and understanding and jlistens as you talk.

Start by describing the basic outline of the situation. Your Inner Expert is very wise and aware, but he or she may have a few questions or may ask you to give more details. Maybe your Inner Expert wants to know what the most important and difficult elements of the situation are for you, and how you feel about the situation and the other parties involved in it. Take about thirty seconds now to explain the situation so that your Inner Expert really understands it. [Thirty-second pause.]

And now that you have finished explaining the situation, your Inner Expert has some answers and suggestions for you. Just listen as he or she tells you what to do. Maybe you have never heard ideas like these before, or maybe you have already thought of these ideas yourself but have not felt sure about them. Just listen very receptively. Don't try to judge or evaluate. For the next sixty seconds, just listen to these ideas as your Inner Expert gives them to you. [Sixty-second pause.]

Now, if you want to, you can ask whether your Inner Expert has any more suggestions for you—or, if there is something you haven't understood, you can ask him or her to elaborate. Again, just listen for the next thirty seconds, and don't try to judge. [Thirty-second pause.]

And now your Inner Expert is finishing his or her answer. You can ask another question if you have one, or if you have another problem or conflict that you're concerned about, you can ask about it, too. This time your Inner Expert's answer will come in the form of something that he or she shows you. You will ask your question, and in response your Inner Expert will lead you away to a different place and show you a screen or a stage, where your answer will appear to you. Maybe the answer will appear as words on a screen, like a headline, or maybe you will see a little drama playing itself out on a stage.

All you have to do is let your Inner Expert lead you to the place where you will see your answer appear in front of you. Just observe. Don't try to plan anything, and don't judge what you are observing. Just receive. Ask your question now and just watch what happens for about a minute. [Sixty-second pause.]

And now your Inner Expert is finishing showing you your answer. So the image in front of you is beginning to fade . . . and now it's gone.

Now your Inner Expert is leading you back to where you first met. Thank your Inner Expert, and know as you say good-bye that you can call on him or her whenever you want, whenever you have a problem or a conflict, or for other reasons—whenever you want some answers. Whenever you call on your Inner Expert, you will be able to either ask a question and be told an answer or have your Inner Expert take you to a place and show you an answer.

Now watch as your Inner Expert leaves. You feel very satisfied, very complete, as you see him or her go.

Now listen, and you will hear a countdown from five to one. The closer you get to the number one, the more you'll be awake and alert. Five. You're waking up. Four. More and more alert. Three. You're coming back to the room where you began this exercise. Two. You're almost back. One. And now you're back. When you're ready, you can open your eyes.

You can adapt the Inner Expert exercise in any number of ways by just changing the questions and changing who you select as your Inner Expert. If you need to choose a conflict style, for example, you can ask your Inner Expert to lead you, in the second part of the exercise, to a place where you will see a movie screen or a stage set with images of yourself using each of the five conflict styles in turn. You can then consider your options in light of what you observe while watching the images of yourself putting each style into action.

SELF-TALK

If you are a less visually oriented person, you may experience your intuition in the form of *self-talk:* a free flow of thoughts or words as you listen internally. It can take the form of hearing a conversation with yourself, much like hearing the words of a teacher or a speaker on the radio. Like visualization, self-talk can be used either as an exercise that you do by yourself or as one that you do in a group (such as when all the members of a work team take turns sharing their individual answers to a question asked of the team as a whole).

Start the self-talk process by getting into a state of deep relaxation, as in visualization, and then begin to ask yourself (or the group) questions. These will be the same kinds of questions that you might ask yourself if you were using your reason alone. The difference is that, in your highly relaxed, receptive state, you will hear the answers from your intuitive mind as your inner voice talks to you. Here are examples of questions you might ask:

What are the underlying causes of this conflict?

Does _____ have a specific motive for taking this particular position? If so, what is it?

What, for me, would be the ideal resolution of this conflict?

What are some possible ways in which this conflict could be resolved?

What can I do to realize these alternatives? *[After you identify each alternative resolution, ask yourself how you can bring it about.]*

In short, generate a series of questions about the nature of the conflict, its causes from the perspectives of the various parties, and alternative ways of resolving it. Then listen receptively to what your inner voice tells you, and write down or tape the responses as you hear them (or immediately afterward).

Your Gut Feeling

As you work with the intuitive techniques, you will also develop your sense of knowing that something is a good or right choice. This is a kind of survival instinct that we all have, akin to an animal's awareness that prey—or a predator—is nearby. We experience a sense of reassurance or comfort when we do what we feel is correct, and we can also sense when something is wrong—like a warning signal of danger that tells us to turn back or proceed with caution. For example, we might sense that implementing someone else's ideas will not be an effective course of action, or that we are about to step into a situation ripe for conflict (as in an office where everyone seems friendly, but there is an underlying tension that no one wants to reveal to others).

Because this kind of inner knowing comes to us as a feeling or a sensation, it's very hard to put it into words for the purposes of a discussion. Our culture also teaches us to tune this inner knowing out and to be externally oriented and rational, following established rules and procedures.

Nevertheless, if you learn to pay attention to your inner knowing, it can supplement your rational views and opinions about what to do in a difficult situation. Ask yourself how you feel when you are comfortable with something. Do you notice a sensation of release or lightness? Alternatively, how do you feel when you're uncomfortable? What signs of discomfort does your body give you—do you feel tension in your shoulder or jaw muscles, for example, or do you experience a tightening in your stomach (where you experience it as a so-called gut feeling)?

RESOURCES

Conflict Resolution

Anderson, K. *Resolving Conflict Sooner: The Powerfully Simple 4 Step Method for Reaching Better Agreements More Easily Plus 100 Useful Tips.* Freedom, Calif.: Crossing Press, 1999.

Axelrod, A., and Holtje, J. *201 Ways to Deal with Difficult People.* New York: McGraw-Hill, 1997.

Borisoff, D., and Victor, D. A. *Conflict Management: A Communication Skills Approach.* Needham Heights, Mass.: Allyn & Bacon, 1997.

Bramson, R. M. *Coping with Difficult Bosses.* New York: Birch Lane Press, 1992.

Bramson, R. M. *Coping with Difficult People.* New York: Ballantine, 1981. (Reissue New York: Dell, 1998.)

Brinkman, R. M. *Dealing with People You Can't Stand: How to Bring Out the Best in People at Their Worst.* New York: McGraw-Hill, 1994.

Brinkman, R. M. *How to Deal with Difficult People,* audiocassette. Boulder, Colo.: Career Track Publications and Fred Pryor Seminars, 1995.

Burton, J. W. *Conflict Resolution: Its Language and Processes.* Lanham, Md.: Scarecrow Press, 1996.

Burton, J. W., and Dukes, F. *Conflict: Practices in Management, Settlement, and Resolution.* Hampshire, England: Macmillan, 1990.

Cahn, D. D., and Lulofs, R. S. *Conflict: From Theory to Action.* Needham, Mass: Allyn & Bacon, forthcoming.

Cava, R. *Difficult People: How to Deal with Impossible Clients, Bosses, and Employees.* Buffalo, N.Y.: Key Porter Books, 1992.

Cornelius, H., and Faire, S. *Everyone Can Win: How to Resolve Conflict.* East Roseville, NSW: Simon & Schuster Australia, 1998.

Costantino, C. A., and Merchant, C. S. *Designing Conflict Management Systems: A Guide to Creating Productive and Healthy Organizations.* San Francisco: Jossey-Bass, 1995.

Davis, E., O'Shea, M., and Fenn, P. (Eds.). *Dispute Resolution and Conflict Management in Construction.* New York: Routledge, 1998.

Elgin, S. H. *How to Disagree without Being Disagreeable: Getting Your Point Across with the Gentle Art of Verbal Self-Defense.* New York: Wiley, 1997.

Foddy, M., et al. (Eds.). *Resolving Social Dilemmas: Dynamic, Structural, and Intergroup Aspects.* San Antonio, Tex.: Psychology Press, 1999.

Folger, J. P., Poole, M. S., and Stutman, R. K. *Working Through Conflict: Strategies for Relationships, Groups, and Organizations.* Reading, Mass: Addison-Wesley, 1996.

Friedman, P. *How to Deal with Difficult People.* Mission, Kans.: Shellrath, 1994.

Grant W. *Resolving Conflicts: How to Turn Conflict into Cooperation.* Boston: Element Books, 1997.

Hall, H. V., and Whitaker, L. C. (Eds.). *Collective Violence: Effective Strategies for Assessing and Interviewing in Fatal Group and Institutional Aggression.* Boca Raton, Fla.: CRC Press, 1999.

Kheel, T. W. *The Key to Conflict Resolution: Proven Methods of Settling Disputes Voluntarily.* New York: Four Walls Eight Windows, 1999.

Kriesberg, L. *Constructive Conflicts: From Escalation to Resolution.* Lanham, Md.: Rowman & Littlefield, 1998.

Levine, S. *Getting to Resolution: Turning Conflict into Collaboration.* San Francisco: Berrett-Koehler, 1998.

Lickson, C. P. *Ironing It Out: Seven Simple Steps to Resolving Conflict.* Menlo Park, Calif.: Crisp Publications, 1996.

Lynch, C. *You Can Work It Out: The Power of Personal Responsibility in Restoring Relationships.* Nashville, Tenn.: Word Publishing, 1999.

Markham, U. *How to Deal with Difficult People.* London: Thorsons, 1988.

Markham, U. *Managing Conflict.* London: Thorsons, 1998.

McDermott, E. P., and Berkeley, A. E. *Alternative Dispute Resolution in the Workplace.* Westport, Conn.: Greenwood Press, 1996.

Miall, H., Ramsbotham, O., and Woodhouse, T. *Contemporary Conflict Resolution: The Prevention, Management and Transformation of Deadly Conflict.* Malden, Mass.: Blackwell, 1999.

Nathan, A., and Steiner, R. *Everything You Need to Know about Conflict Resolution.* New York: Rosen Publishing Group, 1996.

Pirtle, S. *Discovery Time for Cooperation and Conflict Resolution.* Nyack, N.Y.: Creative Response to Conflict, 1998.

Potter-Efron, R. *Working Anger: Preventing and Resolving Conflict on the Job.* Oakland, Calif.: New Harbinger, 1998.

Rothman, J. *Resolving Identity-Based Conflict in Nations, Organizations, and Communities.* San Francisco: Jossey-Bass, 1997.

Sandole, D. J., and van der Merwe, H. *Conflict Resolution Theory and Practice.* Manchester, England: Manchester Univ. Press, 1993.

Schellenberg, J. A. *Conflict Resolution: Theory, Research and Practice.* Albany: State Univ. of New York, 1996.

Scott, G. G. *Resolving Conflict with Others and within Yourself.* Oakland, Calif.: New Harbinger, 1990.

Shister, N. *10 Minute Guide to Negotiating.* Foster City, Calif.: IDG Books Worldwide, 1997.

Shrock-Shenk, C., et al. (Eds.). *Making Peace with Conflict: Practical Skills for Conflict Transformation.* Scottdale, Pa.: Herald Press, 1999.

Singer, L. R. *Settling Disputes: Conflict Resolution in Business, Families, and the Legal System.* Boulder, Colo.: Westview Press, 1994.

Solomon, M. *Working with Difficult People.* Paramus, N.J.: Prentice Hall, 1990.

Stevenin, T. J. *Win/Win Solutions: Resolving Conflict on the Job.* Chicago: Moody Press, 1997.

Stitt, A. J. *Alternative Dispute Resolution for Organizations: How to Design a System for Effective Conflict Resolution.* New York: Wiley, 1998.

Tidwell, A. *Conflict Resolved?: A Critical Assessment of Conflict Resolution.* Herndon, Va.: Books International, 1998.

Tjosvold, D. *Learning to Manage Conflict: Getting People to Work Together Productively.* San Francisco: Jossey-Bass, 1993.

Weeks, D. *The Eight Essential Steps to Conflict Resolution: Preserving Relationships at Work, at Home, and in the Community.* New York: Putnam, 1994.

Weiss, D. H., and Linkemer, B. *How to Deal with Difficult People.* New York: AMA-COM, 1987.

Weiss, D. S. *Beyond the Walls of Conflict: Mutual Gains Negotiating for Unions and Management.* Chicago: Irwin, 1996.

Wiskinski, J. *Resolving Conflicts on the Job.* New York: AMACOM, 1993.

Mediation

Bush, R. A. B. *The Promise of Mediation: Responding to Conflict through Empowerment and Recognition.* San Francisco: Jossey-Bass, 1994.

Beer, J. E., and Stief, E. *The Mediator's Handbook.* New York: New Society, 1997.

Domenici, K. *Mediation: Empowerment in Conflict Management.* Prospect Heights, Ill.: Waveland Press, 1996.

Dunlop, J. T. *Mediation and Arbitration of Employment Disputes.* San Francisco: Jossey-Bass, 1997.

Folberg, J. *Mediation: A Comprehensive Guide to Conflict Resolution.* San Francisco: Jossey-Bass, 1984.

Greenstone, J. L., and Leviton, S. C. *Elements of Mediation.* Pacific Grove, Calif.: Brooks/Cole, 1996.

Kolb, D. M. *When Talk Works: Profiles of Mediators.* San Francisco: Jossey-Bass, 1997.

Moore, C. W. *The Mediation Process: Practical Strategies for Resolving Conflict.* San Francisco: Jossey-Bass, 1996.

Potter, B. A., and Frank, P. *From Conflict to Cooperation: How to Mediate a Dispute.* Berkeley, Calif.: Ronin, 1996.

Rue, N. N. *Everything You Need to Know About Peer Mediation.* New York: Rosen Publishing Group, 1997.

Sorenson, D. L. *Conflict, Resolution, and Mediation for Peer Helpers.* Minneapolis, Minn.: Educational Media, 1992.

Stein, M., et al. *Resolving Conflict Once and for All: A Practical How-To Guide to Mediating Disputes.* Corydon, Ind.: Mediation First Press, 1997.

Cross-Cultural and Community Perspectives on Conflict Resolution

Avruch, K. *Culture and Conflict Resolution.* Herndon, Va.: U.S. Inst. of Peace Press, 1998.

Avruch, K., et. al. *Conflict Resolution: Cross-Cultural Perspectives.* Westport, Conn.: Praeger, 1991.

Dukes, E. F. *Resolving Public Conflict: Transforming Community and Governance (Political Analyses).* Manchester, England: Manchester Univ. Press, 1996.

Fry, D. P., and Bjorkqvist, K. (Eds.). *Cultural Variation in Conflict Resolution.* Mahwah, N. J.: Lawrence Erlbaum Associates, 1996.

Kriesberg, L. *International Conflict Resolution.* New Haven, Conn.: Yale Univ. Press, 1992.

Mills, M. K. (Ed.). *Conflict Resolution and Public Policy.* Westport, Conn.: Greenwood Press, 1990.

Myers, S., and Filner, B. *Resolving Conflict across Cultures: Talking It Out to Mediation.* Amherst, Mass.: Amherst Educational Publishing, 1997.

Ross, M. H. *The Management of Conflict: Interpretations and Interests in Comparative Perspective.* New Haven, Conn.: Yale Univ. Press, 1993.

Rothman, J. *From Confrontation to Cooperation: Resolving Ethnic and Regional Conflict.* Newbury Park, Calif.: Sage, 1992.

Staff Navigators. *Relationships: Resolving Conflict and Building Community.* Colorado Springs, Colo.: NavPress Publishing Group, 1997.

Wolfe, A. W., and Yang, H. (Eds.). *Anthropological Contributions to Conflict Resolution.* Athens: Univ. of Georgia Press, 1996.

INDEX

Accommodating style, of handling conflict, 108–110, 116

active listening: description of, 48; keys to, 49–51

agenda, of individual: description of, 39; hidden. *See* hidden agendas

anger: Exploder personality type, 74–75; holding back versus releasing, 21; how to control, 21–23. *See also* negative emotions

assumptions: checking of, 47–48; faulty, 45–48; forming of, 45; hidden, 45–48

Avoiding style, of handling conflict, 105–108, 116

body language: and identifying hidden agendas, 41; types of, 41

brainstorming: action plan for implementing ideas, 143–144; approaches to, 136, 138; case study example of, 145–146; checklist for, 140; description of, 135; group-based approaches to, 140–143; ideas generated during, 138–143; methods of, 138; self-approaches to, 138–139; when not to use, 137; when to use, 136

By-the-Booker personality type, 85–86

clarity, when communicating, 33, 35–37

Clock Watcher personality type, 84–85

Collaborating style, of handling conflict, 103–105, 113–116

communication: assessment of, 34; benefits of, 31; breakdowns in, 31–33, 36; case study example of, 32–33; clarity and completeness problems in, 33, 35–37; discrepancies between nonverbal and verbal response to, 39; effect of negative emotions on, 31; methods of, 40; and noncommunication-related problems, 37–39; principles of, 33–39; with superiors, 38–39

Competing style, of handling conflict, 100–103, 115–116